ASTROLOGY
FOR TEENS

The Universe Can Tell Us Who We Are and Who We'll Become

Learn to Speak the Language of the Stars to Discover Your Place in the World and Unlock Your Full Potential

WITHDRAWN

Olivia Smith

© **Copyright 2022 Olivia Smith - All rights reserved.**

The content contained within this book may not be reproduced, duplicated or transmitted without direct written permission from the author or the publisher. Under no circumstances will any blame or legal responsibility be held against the publisher, or author, for any damages, reparation, or monetary loss due to the information contained within this book, either directly or indirectly.

Legal Notice:
This book is copyright protected. It is only for personal use. You cannot amend, distribute, sell, use, quote or paraphrase any part, or the content within this book, without the consent of the author or publisher.

Disclaimer Notice:
Please note the information contained within this document is for educational and entertainment purposes only. All effort has been executed to present accurate, up to date, reliable, complete information. No warranties of any kind are declared or implied. Readers acknowledge that the author is not engaged in the rendering of legal, financial, medical or professional advice. The content within this book has been derived from various sources. Please consult a licensed professional before attempting any techniques outlined in this book.

By reading this document, the reader agrees that under no circumstances is the author responsible for any losses, direct or indirect, that are incurred as a result of the use of the information contained within this document, including, but not limited to, errors, omissions, or inaccuracies.

Introduction, 5

What It All Means, 7

Your Chart in Action, 23

Life According to the Zodiac, 31

The 12 Zodiac Signs, 37

Conclusion, 87

From the Author, 89

Introduction

Astrology is the practice of interpreting the location of the stars, the planets, the Sun, and the Moon to predict their influence on our lives. It has a vast history through various cultures and interpretations where it is believed that these celestial bodies hold a strong influence over us and our futures. Some people don't believe in the truth of astrology, but many of them don't take the time to understand the complexity of it all. It is about more than just interpreting the sign that represents the day you were born. Each person has a cosmic map of influences waiting for interpretation. Not only can understanding astrology help you to understand yourself and prepare for your future, but it can also help you to grow into a happier and more fulfilled version of yourself.

Having a grasp on the bigger picture of your own life can make navigating the smaller, more mundane tasks of daily life, like getting through your work for the day or scheduling out your year, a bit easier. Starting may be difficult for you. After all, you'll come face to face with some of your biggest flaws. But with the help of astrology, you'll be able to come to terms with these flaws and accept your imperfections. Recognizing that everything is much bigger and more expansive than you originally believed can put you on the path to accepting yourself as you are. After all, who are we to argue with the divine reign of the stars and planets? Accepting yourself means embracing all parts of you, the good and the bad, and studying your chart can show your weakest and strongest points. Astrology encourages you to work toward reaching a higher sense of being, but also to be easy on yourself when you make a mistake. Perfection is impossible, after all.

If you can embrace the divine, you can begin to take steps toward improving yourself. It goes beyond just understanding that you are a fundamentally flawed person. What are some things you can do to begin working on yourself? You can use your chart to find the best ways to use your strengths to improve yourself. As you practice, it will start to become natural, and you may feel a sense of comfort knowing that there is a pattern to it all. You may even discover hidden traits or talents that you never knew you had, further opening the door for you to grow.

What It All Means

When it comes to understanding astrology and interpreting the stars, the first thing you should know is some of the common terminology. There are a lot of words and phrases that may not make much sense to someone who hasn't begun learning them. So to start, let's break down the basic concepts, words, and influences of the cosmos.

The Big Three

Oftentimes when you ask someone their zodiac sign, they will only have one that they name. And most people know this one right off the bat too! However, there is a lot more than one zodiac sign influencing each person. You have probably met people who are very different from you despite sharing your sign. Or perhaps you've seen posts online that make assumptions based on your sign, but none of them seem to fit you. While we'll cover Birth Charts a bit later, let's talk about what is known as The Big Three. This trio makes up some of your more vital and prominent influences. These specific signs are called the Sun Sign, Moon Sign, and Ascendant.

The sign you most likely know is your Sun Sign. This sign is the core of your being. It represents your ego, your identity, and what kind of role you play in life. It can also give insight into what you may struggle with. Your Sun Sign may not seem like it fits you, as some people don't grow into this sign until they're a bit older. Or, depending on the other signs that influence your Birth Chart, you may be able to step into the role your Sun Sign provides with ease.

Next is your Moon Sign, which is determined by the date, time, and location of your birth. This sign represents your emotions, feelings, and your mood. It is the side of yourself that comes out when you are alone or with close friends and family. Depending on the makeup of your chart, you may find that you identify more with this sign than your Sun Sign. Your Moon Sign heavily impacts your relationships, as being around people who are compatible with your sign will make you feel more at ease.

Astrological Table

SIGNS	APPROX DATES	RULING PLANETS	ENERGY
Aries	Mar 21 – Apr 20	Mars	Day / Inhale
Taurus	Apr 21 – May 20	Venus	Night / Exhale
Gemini	May 21 – June 20	Mercury	Day / Inhale
Cancer	June 21 – Jul 20	Moon	Night / Exhale
Leo	Jul 21 – Aug 20	Sun	Day / Inhale
Virgo	Aug 21 – Sept 20	Mercury	Night / Exhale
Libra	Sept 21 – Oct 20	Venus	Day / Inhale
Scorpio	Oct 21 – Nov 20	Mars – Traditional Pluto – Modern	Night / Exhale
Sagittarius	Nov 21 – Dec 20	Juniper	Day / Inhale
Capricorn	Dec 21 – Jan 20	Saturn	Night / Exhale
Aquarius	Jan 21 – Feb 20	Saturn – Traditional Uranus – Modern	Day / Inhale
Pisces	Feb 21 – Mar 20	Juniper – Traditional Neptune – Modern	Night / Exhale

Finally, is your Ascendant, or what is often called your Rising Sign. This is the sign that was rising into the sky at the moment of your birth. This sign represents how others perceive you and how you present yourself to those around you. It heavily influences your personality as well as your appearance. Your Rising Sign also tends to form the 'mask' that you show to strangers and acquaintances.

Decans

Do you want to know why people born under the same zodiac sign are different? As already mentioned, It takes the entire birth chart to determine the nature of an individual!

There are so many ways to dive further into your astrological personality. While beginners might look to their moon or rising sign, those who are a bit more into their zodiac journey might want to dig into more intricate concepts—like decans (also called "decantes"). Before going into the Four Modalities, let's briefly introduce this interesting method.

Modern astrologers have taken the divisions of the zodiac signs further: They divided the signs and determined rulership; this division is called the decanates. The complete natal chart is 360 degrees, and 12 zodiac signs at 30 degrees each constitute the complete natal chart. Then, each sign has three decans, one for each division of 10 degrees. Each decan has a ruler, and each rules become the sub ruler of the sign or the co-ruler of that sign. So, your decan depends on where your birthday falls within that 30-degree angle: the first ten days of your sign represent the first decan, the second 10 days is the second decan, and the third ten days is the third decan.

Once you are familiar with the Four Elements, it will be much easier to determine the sub-rulers of each decan. Each decan is arranged in the same order as they appear in the zodiac; therefore, each decan is in the same element of the sign itself.

For example, the first decan of Aries is Aries, ruled by Mars. The second decan is Leo, ruled by the Sun, the next fire sign in the zodiac. So the second decan of Aries is ruled by the Sun. The third decan of Aries would be the next fire sign after Leo, which is Sagittarius, ruled by Jupiter. Each decan is of the same Triplicity - the fire element. The first decan of Taurus is Taurus, ruled by Venus. The second decan of Taurus is Virgo, ruled by Mercury. The third decan of Taurus is Capricorn, ruled by Saturn. Each decan is of the same Triplicity - the earth element.

The Four Elements and Three Modalities

The 12 zodiac signs are grouped into the four elements found in the natural world. These are fire, earth, water, and air. These elements work together, balance each other, and exist in harmony within the world. The one tied to your sign can give a bit of insight into your personality traits. Understanding their differences can clue you in as to why

Table of Decans

SIGNS	1 DECAN 0°-9°	2 DECAN 10°-19°	3 DECAN 20°-29°
ARIES	MARS, ARIES	SUN, LEO	JUNIPER, SAGITTARIUS
TAURUS	VENUS, TAURUS	MERCURY, VIRGO	SATURN, CAPRICORN
GEMINI	MERCURY, GEMINI	VENUS, LIBRA	SATURN AND URANUS, AQUARIUS
CANCER	MOON, CANCER	MARS, PLUTO, SCORPIO	JUNIPER AND NEPTUNE, PISCES
LEO	SUN, LEO	JUNIPER, SAGITTARIUS	MARS, ARIES
VIRGO	MERCURY, VIRGO	SATURN, CAPRICORN	VENUS, TAURUS
LIBRA	VENUS, LIBRA	SATURN AND URANUS, AQUARIUS	MERCURY, GEMINI
SCORPIO	MARS AND PLUTO, SCORPIO	JUNIPER AND NEPTUNO, PISCES	MOON, CANCER
SAGITTARIUS	JUNIPER, SAGITTARIUS	MARS, ARIES	SUN, LEO
CAPRICORN	SATURN, CAPRICORN	VENUS, TAURUS	MERCURY, VIRGO
AQUARIUS	SATURN AND URANUS, AQUARIUS	MERCURY, GEMINI	VENUS, LIBRA
PISCES	JUNIPER AND NEPTUNE, PISCES	MOON, CANCER	MARS AND PLUTO, SCORPIO

some people act the way they do. It also helps to understand how some signs can be more compatible than others. For example, signs that share an element tend to understand each other well, despite their differences. Alternatively, some can help to balance one another.

Aries, Leo, and Sagittarius make up the three fire signs. Much as you may expect, they are bright, flashy, and fierce. They can be very enthusiastic and passionate. With high energy and creativity levels, they burn as bright as the Sun. Fire signs prefer to work things out alone and typically have an adventurous and excitable spirit. They enjoy being the center of attention, which is easy to accomplish, considering how charismatic and charming they are. The downside is that their fiery nature can grow out of control if they don't keep a close tab on it. They can become overzealous or even pushy, and many tend to have quite a temper. This may present itself as selfishness or an inflated ego, which can elicit negative reactions from those around them. It's important for fire signs to learn how to channel their energy into more positive and productive things.

As for the earth signs, they are Taurus, Virgo, and Capricorn. These signs tend to be more practical and calm, preferring to think things over rather than making rash decisions. They are hard-working and dedicated, enjoying the physical rewards of their efforts. This could be any material possession that shows their hard-earned success. Overall, earth signs are very reliable and sturdy, tending to be the ones that others know they can come to when they need help. However, they can be incredibly stubborn and set in their ways, refusing to waver from what they know. Earth signs may fear change in their routine, even if they would be better for them. They may also become materialistic or greedy because of their interest in physical possessions. Earth signs can be cautious and more conservative than other signs. They expect those around them to view things the way that they do. They may overlook others involved, as their eyes tend to be focused steadily on the finish line.

The three water signs are Cancer, Scorpio, and Pisces. These signs are the more emotional ones and tend to be very intuitive. Rather than making decisions based on logic, they prefer to focus on their emotions, choosing heart over mind. How things make them feel takes priority in just about everything. These signs can be comforting and connect with others emotionally, making them perfect to confide in when experiencing a difficult emotional situation. Having the ability to understand and process their emotions is vital for them to understand themselves.

They also enjoy the beauty of life and prioritize creativity, making them skilled in the arts. The downside is that water signs can easily become overwhelmed with their emotions, causing significant mood swings. They may take things too personally and end up with hurt feelings, which can evolve into suspicion or distrust. A water sign with no direction may feel like they lack purpose, and should find a way to use their innate emotional skills to ensure they fulfill that desire.

Finally, the air signs consist of Gemini, Libra, and Aquarius. They are far more practical and intellectual people. They are good at working through more abstract problems.

Air signs prefer open and honest communication, including their desire to share their world views with others. They are very rational and prefer logic over emotion. They are also incredibly perceptive. However, if you upset an air sign, they can become cold and harsh. They are a bit flighty and may be quick to leave you behind. Air signs struggle to fit into specific molds, including within their community or workplace. They feel their ideas and plans are too big to fit into such a small space. They have difficulty grounding themselves and understanding the importance of their present selves. They tend to be big talkers, but not doers, and most of their ideas go unused. They have to learn to stick to them and see them through. Not all of their broad concepts and idealistic plans will work out, but those that do will help to fill them with purpose.

Similar to their elemental division, signs are divided into three modalities. These are cardinal, fixed, and mutable. Each modality has a sign from each element within it. Rather than indicating your personality, the modality speaks more to your behavior. They can influence how you react to and approach certain situations. Depending on which part of your Birth Chart is influenced, the modality of that sign can be telling of varying different behaviors.

The cardinal signs are Aries, Cancer, Libra, and Capricorn. Cardinal signs tend to be the doers, the initiators, and the leaders. They are very driven and hard-working people, rarely giving themselves a chance to slow down or slack off. They prefer to be in charge and expect others to follow their lead. They may, however, develop a habit of not finishing the projects that they start. The downside is that the cardinal signs may become overbearing when working in groups. They tend to micromanage others or become controlling of the process. They may even dismiss others, becoming hyperfocused on their own goals. Overall, they have a bright spirit and tend to have lots of projects going on in their life.

Next are the fixed signs, which consist of Taurus, Leo, Scorpio, and Aquarius. As the name implies, they tend to be very steady, focused, and dedicated. They work away at their goals and projects at a set pace and are self-reliant. With how steadfast they are, they also became dependable. Their dedication bleeds into their personal and romantic relationships as well. They will work toward a goal or finish line at their own pace, knowing that they will get the job done no matter what. Their way works, after all! However, they have a habit of believing that their method is the only right way to do things, and can become very stuck in their ways. Others may see them as incredibly stubborn because they refuse to budge from their process. Fixed people are rather opinionated and very resistant to change in their lives.

Finally, the mutable signs are Gemini, Virgo, Sagittarius, and Pisces. Mutable people are far more fluid, thriving in environments with constant change. They prefer to go with the flow and adapt easily to shifts in their environment. They don't mind chaos and are more than willing to try new things. They are also very resourceful, which helps them to fit whatever mold they are trying to fill at that moment. They aren't typically people who will stand their ground, and instead, try to make everyone happy. This desire can

★ WHAT IT ALL MEANS ★

sometimes give others a negative perception of them. They may seem unreliable, dubious, or inconsistent. But the reality is that mutable signs just want to help others. They struggle to nail down ideas and work through them consistently. These signs have a habit of stretching themselves too thin when trying to please others, but they're typically able to snap back after the fact.

The Planets

Beyond your signs, the position of the planets has a heavy influence on you. The location of the planet, the distance between them, and what sign they reside in can all mean different things for you. While the details depend on your Birth Chart, there are some basic aspects that each planet reigns over.

Mercury indicates how you communicate with others as well as how you express yourself. It determines how you work within a group setting and handle problems. It also influences how you convey your ideas and receive information from those around you. Mercury is a major planet on your chart, as it has a significant impact on various parts of your daily life. This planet governs Gemini and Virgo.

Venus is the planet of love, so naturally, it has a heavy influence on the romantic and artistic aspects of your life. Your tastes, love language, and values are a few examples. It also rules over what you desire from romantic relationships. Self-care and spoiling yourself are influenced by Venus as well, ruling over how you love and care for yourself. Venus governs both Taurus and Libra.

Mars rules over action and ambition. Rather than love, this planet reigns over physical attraction. Mars is all about drive. It pushes you to reach for goals, finish what you started, and take that first step. It also indicates aggression and at what point you may become hostile. It governs over Aries.

Jupiter is often associated with growth, as it rules over purpose and freedom. It helps guide you to change and grow as a person, opening your eyes to your broader understanding of yourself. It rules over your ability to understand and learn. Jupiter governs over Sagittarius.

Saturn is the planet of stability and structure. It rules over responsibility and self-control, but also restrictions and limits. It serves to remind you of a sometimes harsh reality of life. Saturn likes to teach you lessons to help you grow and mature. It helps to regulate and discipline you and guides you to understand your stipulations. This planet governs Capricorn.

Uranus rules over a higher sense of being. It speaks to your sense of individuality and guides you to understand your unique quirks. This is the part of you that often doesn't fit into the 'norm' of society. Uranus fuels your more rebellious side. It also governs over Aquarius.

Neptune is the more spiritual planet, as it rules enlightenment, dreams, and intuition. It also tends to fuel your imagination, leading to your daydreams and your more beautiful and creative take on life. Your level of psychic energy is influenced by Neptune. It governs over Pisces.

Pluto pushes you to seek a change, as it often shows what lurks below the surface. This planet influences birth and death, both literally and figuratively. Rebirths and new beginnings are guided by Pluto. As it rules over an entire generation, it often guides you to look deeper and explore past what those before you managed to do. Pluto governs Scorpio.

Table of Major Aspects

PLANT IN THIS SIGNS	LOOKING FOR OPPOSITION IN…	LOOKING FOR SQUARES IN…	LOOKING FOR SEXTILES IN…	LOOKING FOR TRINES IN…
Aries	Libra	Cancer, Capricorn	Gemini, Aquarius	Leo, Sagittarius
Taurus	Scorpio	Leo, Aquarius	Cancer, Pisces	Virgo, Capricorn
Gemini	Sagittarius	Virgo, Pisces	Leo, Aries	Libra, Aquarius
Cancer	Capricorn	Aries, Libra	Virgo, Taurus	Scorpio, Pisces
Leo	Aquarius	Taurus, Scorpio	Gemini, Libra	Aries, Sagittarius
Virgo	Pisces	Gemini, Sagittarius	Cancer, Scorpio	Taurus, Sagittarius
Libra	Aries	Cancer, Capricorn	Leo, Sagittarius	Gemini, Aquarius
Scorpio	Taurus	Leo, Aquarius	Virgo, Capricorn	Cancer, Pisces
Sagittarius	Gemini	Virgo, Pisces	Libra, Aquarius	Aries, Leo
Capricorn	Cancer	Aries, Libra	Scorpio, Pisces	Taurus, Virgo
Aquarius	Leo	Taurus, Scorpio	Aries, Sagittarius	Gemini, Libra
Pisces	Virgo	Gemini, Sagittarius	Taurus, Capricorn	Cancer, Scorpio

The Aspects

In astrology, we map out the planets and stars on a wheel. This is called the wheel of the zodiac. It helps to understand which parts of your chart will be activated by certain planets and signs. As far as aspects go, they are the different angles that planets can form when compared to the other planets around them. These aspects can influence the relationship that the planets share. Their reign over you can depend on what sign they are in and how far they are from the other planets.

A conjunction is made when two planets are around 0° apart. This means that they are so close that their joined influence is heavily reigning over the sign that they are in. This can be great if the two energies can mesh well with one another. It could indicate a very productive time for you. However, if they don't, it can be a more troubling time.

A sextile is when two planets are 60° apart. This angle tends to be a very calm and peaceful interaction between the two planets. It is often a very relaxing time, giving you the perfect opportunity for a break. The downside is that this period will not be productive at all. Don't expect to make major moves or get to working on big projects.

A trine is when two planets are 120° apart. These are considered the best times. They can bring good luck, productivity, and fortune. That's because planets residing within the same element are interacting, bringing a powerful period. The thing to look out for is letting the comfort of this period take over. You may be inclined to take it easy and relax, but this isn't the time. Take advantage of this period to be as productive as you can!

A square refers to a time when two planets are 90° apart. Get ready for a doozy, because these periods tend to be rife with tension. But this shouldn't be immediately written off as a bad thing. If anything, the clash between two planets can spur you on to make an active change in your life. This period will bring challenges forth, but they're ones that you'll be able to overcome with a bit of hard work and dedication. These aspects can lead to resolutions and conclusions, even if they are difficult to achieve.

Opposition occurs when two planets are 180° apart. Or, more plainly, when they are directly across from one another on the wheel. Due to them falling into opposing elements, the two planets can clash. Plus, the distance between them makes it hard to find harmony. So, it will fall upon you to try to balance the influences of the two planets. If you can, this period can go relatively smoothly.

The Houses

The zodiac is divided into 12 sections that are called houses. These houses are associated with specific traits within yourself, the people you interact with, and the environment you live in. Which house the signs and planets were in at the time of your birth also plays a part in the makeup of your chart. Which sections are activated can clue you in on some of your strengths and struggles in life.

The First House is ruled by Aries as well as the planet Mars. This house covers all variations of firsts and aspects of the self. It rules over your childhood, shaped by your earliest memories and first steps in this world. These aspects of your life shape your view of the world around you and heavily influence the person you become. Aspects of your personality and self-expression are also guided by this house. Who you are, and the kind of person you will become, is the core of what this house speaks to.

The Second House is ruled by Taurus and the planet Venus. This house covers various physical and material things around you, including what you can interact with through all five of your senses. But this house also rules over non-material things that you possess. This includes your emotions, ambitions, needs, and self-esteem. The concept of what you value, material or otherwise, is important to this house. The Second House also heavily rules over aspects of finances, such as saving money, incurring debt, and acquiring property.

The Third House is ruled by Gemini and the planet Mercury. This house reigns over communication, including verbal and nonverbal. Talking to someone face to face, texting, and using social media are just a few examples. Close and intimate interactions help communication flow and connects you to those around you. Intelligence is highly revered in the Third House. It helps you communicate your grasp on the world to others. In that same vein, this house reigns over early education, which is when you're taught critical thinking and communication skills. Making spiritual connections is at the core of this house.

The Fourth House is ruled by Cancer and the Moon. This house reigns over foundational aspects of your life, such as the home and family. Having a home gives you a sense of security and safety. We often feel calm and at peace at home, and when we don't, we seek to create our own home that gives us that feeling. But home is not just the physical place that you settle into. It is that welcoming and warm feeling that you long for—for yourself and those you love. Ancestry, heritage, culture, and family traditions are also vital to this house. They heavily influence the feeling of home and help to shape what kind of home you long for. Your parents also play a big role in this, as they influence you in your earliest and most impressionable years. This house also rules over privacy and security, as we often feel safest when we are at home, where we can comfortably be ourselves.

The Fifth House is ruled by Leo and the Sun. This house reigns over all kinds of aspects of creativity and self-expression. When you create something pleasing, it brings a sense of satisfaction and joy. The Fifth House also covers things that can bring you emotional satisfaction, such as romance. Drama, self-expression, and attention are all aspects of life that this house influences. Things like hobbies and games bring us similar feelings of enjoyment. Music, art, dance, theater, and literature are creative forms that this house rules over.

⋆ WHAT IT ALL MEANS ⋆

The Sixth House is ruled by Virgo and the planet Mercury. This house rules over aspects of your health, including exercise, diet, wellness, fitness, and overall healthy ways of living. But it goes beyond just that. A large part of being a healthy and stable person is learning how to handle difficult things when forced to face them. Confronting things that scare or worry you makes you stronger and helps you grow into an emotionally healthier version of yourself. Work and service are also ruled by this house, covering things like employment, training, schedules, and organization. Both the work we do for ourselves and others can leave us fulfilled in different ways. And to keep working in both ways, we have to ensure that our health is well taken care of.

The Seventh House is ruled by Libra and the planet Venus. This house covers various relationships and partnerships that you will experience in life. These can be romantic, familial, or business. They teach unity and cooperation and can help you discover your purpose. Through these relationships, you can accomplish bigger things than you could alone. This house influences various forms of partnership, such as those found in contracts, marriages, and business deals. Even if they don't last forever, many of these partnerships will teach and influence you in some way. The relationships you form will serve to shape you into a more complete version of yourself. Similarly, this house rules over the loss of relationships. How you handle these tense, and sometimes painful, situations will shape your future relationships.

The Eighth House is ruled by Scorpio and both Mars and Pluto. This house covers deeper aspects of relationships, including your relationship with the world and yourself. It influences intimacy, birth and death, and transformations. You will experience many highs and lows in life, and in a way, many figurative births and deaths. Be open to these shifts, as they are a part of life, and necessary steps to discover more about yourself. It also covers financial and emotional support. They both feed into the various relationships you form and how much good and harm they may do. Learning how to handle them in these relationships can lead you to the rebirth and new life you need.

The Ninth House is ruled by Sagittarius and the planet Jupiter. This house rules over the higher mind and broader, philosophical concepts. Your need and desire to understand your place in the universe are included. You may decide to pursue further education to learn more or dream of traveling so you can experience foreign cultures and concepts. Both are ways of expanding your mind and your beliefs. Ideas like psychology, philosophy, ethics, spirituality, and religion are all ruled by this house. These ideas are designed to expand your mind and understanding of the world. It also covers the creation and following of laws. Having a balance of laws and higher thinking can lead to a positive progressive society.

The Tenth House is ruled by Capricorn and the planet Saturn. This house speaks to your place within society and your groups, which can include social, workplace, and educational. Fame, status, and achievement are all under this house. The ambitions and goals you have set for yourself tend to be vital to your growth within your environment. These naturally go hand in hand with your status, meaning they fall under the Tenth House. How you handle the responsibility you're given is involved as well. After all, it can be used to benefit society as a whole, but not everyone is expected to make massive progressive changes to their environment. But positive change on a smaller scale is still very possible.

The Eleventh House is ruled by Aquarius and the planets Saturn and Uranus. This house is all about friendships, groups, and teams. This can cover all sorts of social groups you are a part of. More specifically, this house covers the role you serve within these groups, and how this position helps you to grow and learn. Working with your friends toward a shared goal can help you achieve it more easily. It also gives you people to celebrate with. The power of a collective force is vital to achieving great things. Thus, this house also covers humanitarian and social acts. The Eleventh House also reigns over what kind of person and friend you tend to be when in these groups. This influences the type of people that you seek out.

The Twelfth House is ruled by Pisces as well as the planets Jupiter and Neptune. As the last house, this one rules over various endings. Closing deals, concluding chapters of your life, and old age are some things that it includes. It also covers many aspects of the subconscious. Your fears, secrets, worries, sorrows, and failures all reside here. The subconscious can help you cope with them, but can also hide deeply buried secrets from you and others. All of this boils down to the concept of karma. How does one react when faced with everything they hid in their subconscious? This can help you to learn valuable life lessons, and close a chapter in your life before taking the next step. This house can aid you in finding closure in emotional and spiritual manners, which is key to your growth as a person.

North and South Nodes

Unlike the planets, the nodes are not physically present in the sky. Rather, when we refer to the nodes, we mean the point where the sun and moon pass by one another. These points are where eclipses can occur, as they can only happen when the sun and moon are aligned. There are two points where this can happen, and thus, two nodes which separately influence your Birth Chart. These are the North Node and the South Node.

The North Node is said to represent aspects of your future. How you're destined to grow, what you need to become the best version of yourself, or even your life's purpose and desires can be shaped by this aspect. Understanding your own North Node can help you discover what parts of yourself you can work on. This isn't a bad thing, as even though doing so can make you nervous and uncomfortable, working on yourself will only bring you a sense of peace, happiness, and fulfillment. Learning how to grow and understand the necessity of it will help you along your path of knowing yourself.

On the other hand, the South Node represents aspects of your past. It influences your comfort zone and the parts of your life you already inhabit. These are parts of your life

☆ WHAT IT ALL MEANS ☆

that you are already skilled at. But if you stick within these areas, you are often left feeling bored and unfulfilled. Your South Node is a way for you to get to the destiny you have laid out before you. Loosening your grip on these parts of yourself can be difficult, as it can be comforting to stick to what you know. But change is necessary if you want to grow.

If your North Node resides in Aries, then your South Node is in Libra. Your nodes are pushing you to try to step into a leadership role more often. You have to learn to stop putting the needs of others above your own all the time. Also, standing up for yourself is another lesson you'll need to learn. This may cause conflict, but it's the best way for you to grow. You likely feel comfortable trying to fly under the radar and take the safer path, but constantly defaulting to compromise will not allow you to grow as a person.

If your North Node is in Taurus, then your South Node is in Scorpio. They are calling for you to embrace the luxuries of life and have a more material-focused mindset. You should practice self-care often, as it is not only pleasant, but a necessity at times. You are likely more comfortable relying on your feelings and intuitions, but this will not lead to the productivity that you are being pulled toward. You'll have to learn to ground yourself and remember to embrace what is happening around you.

If your North Node is within Gemini, then your South Node resides in Sagittarius. You are being pulled to establish roots and settle into a palace that you can call home. Embrace deeper relationships and relish in the mundaneness of small talk. This may be difficult for you, as you are likely more comfortable floating from place to place. You also tend to prefer philosophy over reality. But settling into and embracing the warmth of home will show you the true brilliance that life has to offer.

If your North Node is in Cancer, then your South Node is within Capricorn. You are being called to embrace a more nurturing take on life. Focus more on healing, growing, and understanding the people and places around you. You may find more comfort in residing within your mind and planning everything in meticulous detail. But instead, you should be embracing your heart. Understanding the rooted desires of your own heart and the hearts of your loved ones can allow you to embrace your calling to be a healer and caregiver.

If your North Node resides in Leo, then your South Node is within Aquarius. You are drawn toward the spotlight. Embrace your uniqueness and charm and allow yourself to glow from the praise of those around you. You probably find comfort in relying on others and working in a larger group setting. Perhaps you believe that a collective approach will be more productive. But you won't truly shine if you are lost among the faces. That Leo North Node is pushing you to strike out on your own.

If your North Node is in Virgo, then your South Node resides in Pisces. Your North Node is indicating that you must learn to understand what you need to thrive. Embrace healthier living, establish routines, and plan for the future. Even if you don't make it to perfection, you should learn to set actual and attainable goals for yourself to reach the place that you want to be. You may find more comfort in fluidly moving through life and just letting things be. But it will take an active effort for you to reach your goals.

If your North Node is within Libra, then your South Node is in Aries. One of the biggest lessons you will need to learn is compromise. Seek out harmony with those around you and embrace the beauty of the unique people you encounter. You're probably more comfortable as a leader and may often default to believing that your way of doing things is the right way. But allowing others to step up and listening to their different perspectives will bring you true growth.

If your North Node is in Scorpio, then your South Node is in Taurus. You are being pulled toward the depths of your mind and heart to explore the fascinating mysteries of life. You'll have to learn to make deeper connections with people, embracing their perspectives. You will have to learn to let go of the more physical aspects of life, which likely feel more natural to you. Instead, rely on your spirituality and grow to discover your higher self.

If your North Node resides in Sagittarius, then your South Node is in Gemini. Your nodes are pulling you to explore the world and experience the vastly different cultures of other places and people. Travel far and wide, meet new people every day, and face it all with a positive mindset. You may feel more compelled to stick to your roots and remain close at home. But this exploration is what you need to open your eyes to the vast world around you. The lessons you learn and things you will experience will help you grow exponentially.

If your North Node is within Capricorn, then your South Node is in Cancer. You are being called to embrace your well-being. This can include learning how to set boundaries, setting your goals, and making progress on them. Your ambitions and desires are important and you'll need to learn to embrace that and allow yourself to pursue them. You would likely prefer to help others, allowing your own needs to suffer while you tuck away in the safety of your bubble. But you won't feel truly fulfilled if you don't embrace what you want in life.

If your North Node is in Aquarius, then your South Node is in Leo. They are pushing you to become part of the collective. Draw on your abilities and harness them to help the greater good. You'll have to learn to be comfortable being just a face in the crowd and find the joy in bettering your community. You likely prefer to be the center of attention and would much rather just do the things that would benefit you. But you will experience a kind of an awakening when you realize just how you feel when you learn to lift and empower those around you.

If your North Node resides in Pisces, then your South Node is within Virgo. You are being called to embrace the spiritual side of life. Let go of a rigid structure and allow yourself to go with the twists and turns you face. You'll have to learn to embrace your emotions and rely less on analytics. You likely feel more comfortable with extensive scheduling and looking at everything through a critical lens. But you will feel a true sense of happiness when you can learn to forgo that for a lighter, freer approach to life.

The Moon

Because the Moon makes up part of your Big Three, it's no surprise that it has a significant influence on your daily life. But not only does it guide you, but the different phases that it passes through do as well. The Moon guides our emotions, and as it changes, so do your feelings. You can easily use this to your advantage though. It just takes understanding what each phase means and then using that to decide how to approach each day.

When the New Moon is in the sky, it is time for beginnings. This will be the perfect time for you to plan out the kinds of things that you want to achieve within the coming weeks of the moon cycle. These can be personal goals of various degrees, so long as they are important to you. Manifest what you want to achieve by writing it down and planning for it.

The Waxing Crescent Moon rises after the New Moon. During this period, you should begin to bring the plans that you set to life. This will be a productive and happy period as you take the first steps toward the intentions you set. Meditating during this time can help

Your Chart in Action

As mentioned before, significantly more goes into your astrological makeup than just your Sun Sign. Each person has a unique Birth Chart that shapes various influences. Where certain signs and planets are in the sky the moment you are born determines said influences. Your Birth Chart serves as a guide to show you what the sky looked like at that moment. Getting your chart is pretty easy. There are plenty of calculators online that you can use. All you need to know is the exact date, time, and location of your birth. Those need to be precise, as certain parts of your chart only remain within one sign for a very brief time. We've discussed at length how different signs and planets can influence you, so your next step is to delve into more detail. What, exactly do they mean for your Birth Chart?

Mercury Retrograde

No matter how much about astrology you know, you've likely heard about Mercury going into retrograde. But what does that even mean, and why does it seem like such a big deal? Firstly, when we say that a planet is "in retrograde," it means that the planet appears as if it is moving backward. Of course, it isn't actually, but due to the speed of Earth's rotation and the orbit of said planet, it makes it look like it is. When this happens, whatever that planet rules over can be thrown off.

So why is Mercury's retrograde such a big deal, even though every planet goes into retrograde at some point? That's because Mercury rules over all aspects of communication, including technology and travel. It is known for causing travel plans to be canceled, difficulty in communicating with others, or even frozen or glitchy tech. This can be frustrating, especially if you're a very busy person with a hectic schedule. It may feel like absolutely nothing is going right. On top of that, Mercury goes into retrograde fairly often. It happens around every three or four months, and can last for three whole weeks! This may leave you feeling as though Mercury is constantly interfering with your life.

A retrograde should not be seen as a bad thing however, even if it does get on your nerves. Mercury going into retrograde is an attempt to force you to take a breather. Especially in current times, as we live in an era where we're expected to constantly be hustling or working. It leaves very little time to stop and relax. It's the perfect time to take a moment to reassess things. Maybe you feel the urge to reconnect with an old friend or you revisit and revise a business plan. Mercury's retrograde is a good period for you to reflect, rather than endlessly pushing forward.

Chiron

Chiron is what is known as the "wounded healer" within astrology. It is currently classified as either a small planet or a comet and has a fairly strange orbital pattern. Chiron is believed to represent the deep, heavy emotional traumas that we have a difficult time healing from. These traumas will often come from childhood, as they are hard to heal from and process at such an age. Or, this can be a karmic level of pain that you may still carry from past lives. Healing this wound is complicated, but very rewarding if you can manage it. Chiron's location on your chart will indicate areas that require a deep level of healing. It can also indicate things you struggle with and how you handle and express those feelings. To use Chiron to your advantage, you have to be willing to work through a difficult emotional healing process.

Saturn Return

When referring to the return of Saturn, it quite literally means when Saturn returns to the exact place, sign, and house that it was in when you were born. This happens about every 30 years, which means it can happen a few times within your lifetime. It tends to remain there for about two or three years, though the effects can show themselves prior and linger for a time afterward. During this period, you may have a difficult time that pushes you to question your life purpose. You may go through a kind of existential crisis and question what kind of legacy you're living or what you'll leave behind. While stressful and overwhelming, this is also the perfect time for personal growth and expansion. It may be the start of the next phase of your life where you begin to feel the weight of responsibility on your shoulders. This period shouldn't be seen as a bad thing, even if it is a lot to handle at the moment. But if you can truly rise to the occasion, you will come out the other side a stronger and wiser person

Indicators of Success

Success in anything takes hard work and effort. It takes a lot of skills and understanding that you need to develop to gain the success you're looking for. However, some people tend to be more naturally inclined and skilled at it than others. Here are a few things you can look out for on your Birth Chart to know if you're one of them.

Sun sextile Midheaven indicates great success and recognition of your work. When you're first starting, your higher-ups will likely notice you and possibly even take you under their wing. You may grow to become just as influential and successful as them within your career.

Sun sextile Jupiter means that you'll likely have your fair share of connections, lucky breaks, friends in high places, and open doors throughout your life. Your generosity to others will also lead to your success and prosperity. The more you give, the more you get back.

The Sun opposite Jupiter indicates that you have a habit of conjuring big dreams and lofty goals for yourself. And you have the confidence to back them up. Your high spirit, desire, and drive will bring success your way. You are likely to prosper in business exploits.

Mars sextile Saturn likely reflects your hard work and dedication to your goals. You are constantly putting in your best effort, even when things get tough, and are probably a very responsible person. And despite the success that comes from this work, you are often humble about it.

Mercury square Jupiter means that you have quite a few traits that foreshadow a successful career in business. You have a vast amount of ideas, incredible foresight, and the instincts to make it all happen.

Mars opposite Jupiter indicates an adventurous spirit and the initiative to get things done. You will thrive in a competitive environment as higher stakes push you even further toward your goals. You will likely do well in both business and sports.

Jupiter conjunct Midheaven usually means that you have big plans and will aspire to do something great in this world. With both your personal goals and your ambitions to make a bigger impact within society, you will experience significant success in both. You may even grow to be a very influential person within your community.

Jupiter conjunct Pluto speaks for your desire to aim for the top. You tend to seek out the right circles to join to get to where you want to be. You have a knack for finding the best opportunities and you will likely grow to be both successful and influential.

Jupiter sextile Midheaven tends to indicate that your path to success will be smoother than most people's. You have probably been supported emotionally, financially, or maybe both, since an early age, and you don't hesitate to seek the help of friends when you reach for a goal. Whatever you set your mind to, it will likely be very lucrative.

Jupiter trine Midheaven means that recognition and success tend to come easily for you. You have all kinds of opportunities at your doorstep, sometimes even more than you can take on. Your bright and positive outlook plays a big factor in this, as does your desire to make a difference.

Jupiter trine Pluto indicates that you are fairly aware of the moves you're making and the success they will draw. You know how to find success with your wide perspective and ability to pick up good opportunities. You will likely be very successful in your career.

Jupiter square Pluto means you have high expectations for yourself, and won't be satisfied until you reach those goals. You likely have connections with successful people and aren't afraid to use that relationship to your benefit. You know how to pick out a great opportunity and are quick to act when the time is right.

Your Life's Purpose

If you are ever left wondering what you are destined to do in life, you can refer to your Birth Chart to get a good idea. It comes down to what house your Sun Sign falls under. Because this sign represents the core of your being, the house it is in can represent what path you are destined to take in life.

If your Sun Sign resides within the First House, your life purpose is focused on aspects of yourself, including your identity and personality. You likely have a strong passion to follow whatever dream you have, and it tends to be a big and passionate one. You may be destined to grow your own business, be your own boss, and strike out as an entrepreneur. Or you could be inclined to leave your mark on the world, pursuing a career as a doctor, police officer, or even an athlete. Whatever you decide, it will involve establishing yourself as a unique individual.

If your Sun Sign falls in the Second House, your life purpose is more involved with money and success. You will likely pursue something that sticks close to your values. Naturally, you will likely pursue a career that will allow you to gather wealth and possessions. A realtor is a good example of this. Alternatively, you may be drawn more to a career that resonates with your beliefs while also showcasing your talents, such as being an artist or musician.

If your Sun Sign is found within the Third House, your purpose involves communication and education. You may feel a desire to seek out more information to broaden your mind, or new and innovative ways to communicate with others. Pursuing a career as a teacher or a professor would allow you to become educated while also educating others. Or you could choose to become a writer or a journalist to share your thoughts with the world. If you enjoy the idea of exploration, a career that lets you visit different places and experience new things may be a better choice.

⁕ YOUR CHART IN ACTION ⁕

If your Sun Sign resides in the Fourth House, your purpose is more involved with family, the home, and nurturing. You may feel compelled to pursue something that you are emotionally invested in. You likely want to share your nurturing nature with others, drawing you toward careers that allow you to do just that. This could be a nurse, teacher, psychologist, caretaker, or chef, just to name a few examples. You desire to connect with others on a deep level, leading to your destiny to care for and help people.

If your Sun Sign is within the Fifth House, your purpose is focused on creativity and self-expression. You probably enjoy the idea of pursuing a career that you are passionate about. This can draw you to a creative career, including the arts and acting, where you can be expressive and passionate. Or you may be more inclined to lead others. You may even find being in a leadership position very natural. As such, you might be interested in careers within a business, the medical field, or even in the military.

If your Sun Sign resides in the Sixth House, your life purpose instead will require you to invest yourself and work tirelessly in your career. You are likely a practical person who can work well when in a crisis. You also enjoy helping others, which can lead to careers within the medical field or commercial work. You likely have several talents and may decide instead to pursue one of those, allowing you to hone and share your skills within whatever field you choose.

If your Sun Sign falls within the Seventh House, your purpose may be more focused on pursuing the arts or your bonds with other people. You may seek out justice and diplomacy, which can lead to a career in law or politics. If you are inclined toward this path, you likely favor fairness and equality above most things. Or, you may pursue your passions around various art forms, being drawn to careers in more creative fields. No matter what you choose, you seek out relationships that you can form with others, so you are destined to work in an environment with various colleagues.

If your Sun Sign is in the Eight House, your purpose is founded more on investigating and researching. You may be drawn to the darker, more hidden aspects of life. This can lead you to a career in psychology, yoga, or various metaphysical practices. You tend to be more interested in meaningful things and may feel inclined to become a healer of some kind, whether it be physical, mental, or spiritual. You seek to restore and revitalize people who may need your help.

If your Sun Sign resides in the Ninth House, your purpose is more focused on exploring and discovering truth through education. You likely want the freedom to travel and see the world, believing these experiences will help you expand your mind and spirit. You may seek out a career that allows you that freedom, such as a pilot, working at sea, or taking up a creative job that doesn't keep you in one place. Or, you may feel inclined to share what you have learned with others, leading you to pursue a career as a judge or perhaps a leader of some kind. You may end up living in and visiting different countries in your life.

If your Sun Sign is within the Tenth House, your purpose is to pour all of your dedication and energy into being the very best in your career. You likely flourish as a leader and tend to be very organized and practical. You may choose to build your own business or aim for the executive position at an established company. Either way, you're climbing to the top. You prefer jobs that push you to work hard and reward you for your efforts. But you will also likely be inclined to help your community in the process. Not only do you want to succeed, but you want society to as well.

If your Sun Sign falls in the Eleventh House, your purpose is more intellectually focused. You likely have the drive to improve your community or even society. This can cause you to pursue a future as a humanitarian or an inventor. You may also be more focused on making a difference in personal lives rather than the bigger picture. This can draw you toward a career as a professor, psychologist, or counselor. You tend to thrive in social situations and want to help those around you. Making a difference at some scale is likely very important to you.

Finally, if your Sun Sign resides in the Twelfth House, your purpose is tied to providing a service to others, especially those who aren't as fortunate as you. Naturally, you may pursue a career that helps people, such as working within institutions or hospitals. You also likely enjoy beauty and creative expression, so you may be more inclined to follow that path to a career. Pursuing arts and music allows you to express yourself and share that beauty with others. Alternatively, you could feel a higher, more spiritual calling and decide to pursue a career in therapy or even your religious practice.

Finding Joy

Happiness comes from all sorts of things in our lives, and what brings each of us joy can vary significantly. But did you know that you can also look to your Birth Chart to gain insight into what can make you the happiest? To do so, you should first look at the location of Venus on your chart. Depending on what sign it is in, it can indicate areas in life that can make you happy. On top of that, you should look at the placement of Jupiter as well. This planet can indicate things that you have a natural inclination toward and will excite you.

If your Venus resides in a fire sign, you will find joy in physical activity. This includes working out, going on walks or jogging, or any other physical way to exert energy. Alternatively, things associated with fire can also make you happy. Perhaps try to cook or grill more or light a few candles around your house. These things can help bring you a sort of pleasantness on a rough day.

If your Venus is in an earth sign, you can bring a bit of joy into your life through material objects. You can decorate your room with new, cute posters, get some fun and colorful school supplies, or even get new clothes. Whichever physical objects you enjoy the most, having them around will cheer you up for sure. You also tend to be more sensitive when it comes to your senses. So, using things such as a diffuser can help bring you calm.

If your Venus is in an air sign, you will find joy in socializing with others. Having active and up-to-date social media profiles, a nice phone, and even a good camera will help ensure you can stay connected. Going out and spending time with your friends, as well as meeting new people, will make you undeniably happy. If you connect more with people online, buying a good webcam and microphone can help you to stay connected.

If your Venus falls within a water sign, then anything that reassures you can also bring you a boost of happiness. These signs tend to be emotional, so surrounding yourself with people who make you feel loved will bring you great joy. Or you can take the time to look back on fond memories and physical reminders of those times. Decorating your space with photos and mementos of the times with people you love will help you feel peaceful and joyful.

If your Jupiter is in a fire sign, you can find excitement in the prospect of new adventures and ideas. While you can't always go on trips at the drop of a hat, planning them down to the smallest detail will bring you a kind of joy. You can always go out and visit more local areas as well. After all, exploring a new place that isn't as far away and exciting as the places you dream of can still fulfill that desire.

If your Jupiter resides in an earth sign, you can find excitement through creating things or making money. Perhaps there's been a project or hobby you've wanted to pick up, or even a business you had an interest in starting. Anything that you can methodically organize and plan out will excite you for the result. Being able to accomplish something and have tangible results can make you feel a sense of refreshment and happiness.

If your Jupiter falls within an air sign, new ideas and information bring you excitement. Find informational shows or podcasts that you can devote some time to, or go out and add some books to your collection. You'll find happiness whenever you're getting new and interesting information. You should also seek out friends and acquaintances who you can chat with. Not only is getting to talk with them enjoyable to you, but you also get excitement from exchanging information and experiences with others.

If your Jupiter is in a water sign, using your intuitive and empathetic nature will bring you excitement. Connect with things that make you feel more in touch with your emotions and bring you a sort of peaceful feeling. Due to this nature, however, you have a habit of attracting different energies depending on what mood you're in. So you always want to ensure you're taking care of your physical and mental well-being to attract positive, pleasant energy to you.

Sibling Relationships

The relationship you have with your siblings can also be influenced by your Birth Chart. While some of these bonds seem to come easily, others are full of tension and rivalry. Your chart can show you where those relationships may flourish, and where they may suffer. But they don't have to remain that way. It's up to you and your siblings to work through any bumps along the way to have a successful familial relationship.

To start with, your Eleventh House represents elder siblings, so if it is strong, then you'll have a strong bond with older siblings. The Eighth House represents younger siblings, so having a strong one on your chart means you will be close with them. If Mars and Mercury are strong and placed well on your chart, they could indicate strong sibling bonds. However, if they are weaker, you may have more strained relationships with them. Mars is also a bit of a special case. If it's overpowering within your chart, it may indicate rivalry.

If your Saturn is located within your Third House, it could indicate some sort of distance between yourself and a sibling. This could be an emotional distance or a literal, physical one. Having your Sun, Moon, Venus, Mars, or Jupiter within your Third House can indicate a stronger sibling bond. Alternatively, if your Moon is within the Sixth, Eighth, or Twelfth Houses, it can mean rivalry with a sibling. Your Moon sign can also strongly influence your sibling relationships. This sign can shape what kind of sibling you are to them, which can be good or bad depending on what it is. The same could be said about your sibling's Moon sign.

Money and Wealth

When it comes to looking to your chart for signs of wealth and financial abundance, it can become a bit more complicated. Several influences could indicate financial prosperity.

For starters, there are a few houses to look out for. You'll have to take note of the planets within these houses, their aspects, what is ruling this house, within what sign, and what signs could be on the cusp of the house. These various influences can alter how you interpret and understand their indication of wealth. What you find within the Second House can indicate the future of your wealth. The Eighth House can hint toward conjoined wealth found within a partnership or union. And finally, you have the Eleventh House, which can indicate your wealth gained through working and your career.

The location of specific planets is also important. For example, Venus, who naturally rules over the Second House, and Jupiter, which influences growth, are important influences. Any planets that reside within the Second and Eighth Houses should also be noted, due to how heavily these houses can influence aspects of wealth. The location and influence of Saturn and Mars also play a part. While not directly connected to money, they have reign over your structure and ambition respectively. How you handle these things in your life can affect how you go about accumulating wealth.

Life According to the Zodiac

Now that you understand your Birth Chart and how to use it, you're probably wondering how your signs are affecting your life. The compatibility of the planets and stars not only influences your traits, but they also reign over your everyday life, your relationships, and all aspects of your future. Life may seem overwhelming at times, but for many questions, you can turn to the stars for help. First, we'll cover a few basic and overarching concepts that can help you through everyday life, no matter what's on your Birth Chart. Then, in the following chapters, we'll get a bit more sign specific.

Planning Your Year

The cosmos is a powerful force and will continue to influence your daily life no matter what sky you were born under. A good way to use that to your benefit is to use its influence to plan your routine. If you know what to look for, you'll be able to decide when to make major decisions, when to avoid efforts toward productivity, and what the most successful periods will be for you.

Firstly, you will want to check to see when each planet will be going into retrograde. Depending on which planet it is, there will be specific activities to avoid during those times. There is also what is known as "retrograde season," which is a period in time when multiple planets will go into retrograde. These are times in which you shouldn't take any major steps in your career or schooling. These can change, depending on the year, so it's important to look up the time frames as you're making plans for a new year.

Another thing to track is the pattern of the moon cycle. Specifically, focus on the full and new moons. Depending on when they rise, they can activate different parts of your Birth Chart. Studying this relationship can help you to plan for the best and worst times to make major changes in your life. Keep an eye out for any moments when the full moon may be activating a natal planet, as this can indicate a productive and intense period. The best way to go about this is to list each full and new moon for the upcoming year and note which parts of your chart the moon will activate. You can plan around them to make the most of the energy they will create.

Finally, you should run what is called a Transit Chart. This chart will help you to track when certain parts of your natal chart will be activated, and by which planet. Looking at the slower-moving planets, you can plan for major events for the year. Alternatively, faster moving planets can help you to prepare for upcoming weeks and months.

Romantic Compatibility

You've probably seen plenty of online posts and articles talking about the most compatible signs. And while there may be some reality to that, it doesn't mean that you're destined to fall in love with one specific sign. Arguably, it's very possible to fall in love with any sign! You just have to understand how different and similar your energies are. The biggest indication of this is how far apart your signs are on the wheel of the horoscope. This distance can either cause harmony or tension between you and the other person. Understanding the compatibility you may share with other signs can give better insight into past, current, and even future relationships. Who knows? Maybe some of those relationships served to help you understand something more about yourself.

When it comes to loving someone who shares the same sign as you, you probably end up handling qualities that are similar to your own. A relationship like this is all founded on the idea of self-acceptance. If you have come to love and understand yourself, and even all of your flaws, then you may find it easy to love someone else who shares similar traits. If you have not, however, then this relationship may be what forces you to come to terms with your flaws and quirks. After all, if you love someone else who is similar to you, then what's stopping you from pouring that same love onto yourself?

If you're romancing someone whose sign is right next to yours, there is likely a significant amount of friction between the two of you. This can lead to a volatile, hot and cold, back and forth kind of relationship. These relationships can lead to a lot of sometimes painful growth. Even if you don't want to accept it, you will learn a lot from them. They can push you out of your comfort zone and make you face the kinds of qualities you may dislike. It may also force you to learn how to stand up for yourself and help you to find your voice. These relationships tend to lead to deep healing and growth. But they also have the potential to end in a difficult and painful breakup.

It can seem easy to date someone who is two signs away from yours. You're usually compatible and have a lot of things in common. These can range from simple things, like taste in movies and books, to bigger picture things, such as desires for your futures. A relationship like this is founded on the idea of open communication and a bond of friendship. This relationship may teach you to openly and directly communicate your wants and needs, and how to listen to those of your partner. While this kind of relationship is easy to start, it may become difficult to keep going. It takes effort to keep the romance alive in a comfortable relationship, and that's an important lesson you will likely learn from loving someone with this sign.

The space between you and someone three signs away creates a harsh, square angle. This leaves room for intense giving and taking within the relationship. This can be difficult, as it can bring up painful reminders of traumas that you still carry, especially if they have been caused by a negative relationship with your parents. It can be a blessing in disguise, as the partnership you have can help you work through the issues and burdens you are carrying. This relationship will be a difficult one due to conflicting ideas and opinions. You may clash often and have a nearly constant power struggle. One of the biggest things you can take away from this relationship is learning how to compromise. It can teach you how to resolve conflict and work with people with personalities that clash with yours. Perhaps you can find that perfect balance with them and become quite the power couple.

If you're in a relationship with someone four signs away from yours, then that means you have one major thing in common: your element. Sharing this aspect of your signs can bring a rather peaceful and understanding relationship. You both seem to understand each other on a deep level, and you may even find that you don't have to explain why you are the way you are. So what can you learn from a relationship like this? Well, a lot about yourself. Being with someone who understands you so easily allows you to be more in touch with your true self. You can learn how to be comfortable in your skin and how to let your walls down and just relax. You'll also experience how it feels to be known and understood as well as the importance of having a partner who is also a friend.

Astrologically speaking, you don't tend to have a whole lot in common with someone whose sign is five away from yours. So being in a relationship with them can seem like the best partnership in the world or the absolute worst. But the connection you have likely extends in a very deep, intimate way. You may even be drawn to one another to heal a sort of karmic weight that you carry. To make a relationship like this work, you'll have to make significant adjustments and potentially compromise with them about some things, which is a major lesson you can take away. This partnership can help you to learn how to be selfless, how to give, and how to change. Understanding this allows you to mesh with someone who is quite different from yourself. So long as you are careful not to lose yourself, these lessons can help you to grow as a person.

These signs are the ones who are on the complete opposite side of the wheel compared to yours. Despite that, you will likely have more in common than you may expect. You tend to challenge one another, pushing each other to be better people. You may feel a greater weight of expectation on your shoulders. The relationship can force you to step back and take in the bigger picture, keeping you from focusing too hard on specific details. It may even open your eyes to what meaning your life holds. You tend to complement one another fairly well and can become quite a powerful pair, even finding ways to balance each other. A relationship with an opposite sign can be uncomfortable and difficult at first, but it can also cause you to grow as a person.

Compatible Signs Chart

SIGNS	COMPATIBLE SIGNS	COMPLEMENTARY SIGNS	INCOMPATIBLE SIGNS
ARIES	Leo, Sagittarius	Gemini, Aquarius	Virgo, Scorpio
TAURUS	Virgo, Capricorn	Cancer, Pisces	Libra, Sagittarius
GEMINI	Libra, Aquarius	Leo, Aries	Scorpio, Capricorn
CANCER	Scorpio, Pisces	Taurus, Virgo	Sagittarius, Aquarius
LEO	Aries, Sagittarius	Libra, Gemini	Capricorn, Pisces
VIRGO	Capricorn, Taurus	Scorpio, Cancer	Aries, Aquarius
LIBRA	Gemini, Aquarius	Sagittarius, Leo	Taurus, Pisces
SCORPIO	Cancer, Pisces	Virgo, Capricorn	Gemini, Aries
SAGITTARIUS	Aries, Leo	Libra, Aquarius	Taurus, Cancer
CAPRICORN	Taurus, Virgo	Pisces, Scorpio,	Gemini, Leo
AQUARIUS	Gemini, Libra	Aries, Sagittarius	Cancer, Virgo
PISCES	Cancer, Scorpio	Taurus, Capricorn	Leo, Libra

FAMILY MATTERS

Depending on the size of your family, you probably live with people who have different signs than yours. You likely have widely different Birth Charts from most of your family members. This can make conflict inevitable and your relationships difficult to navigate at times. Understanding where they may be coming from, and how you can properly navigate responding to them, can make your home life at least a bit more tolerable. If you know the element of their Sun sign, you can start to understand how they handle their family relationships and dynamics.

The fire signs tend to be warm and bright, but they also have a kind of ferocity to them. They are the ones who initiate family dinners or they're your extended relatives who are always trying to set up big family events. They'll also be the family members who go out of their way to check on you. They're typically the ones who try to keep the family bond strong. However, they also tend to come off as authoritative and bossy, as they can get fiery and passionate about things easily. Fire signs also have a habit of speaking before thinking, which can lead them to say rather harsh or even insulting things.

The earth signs are more grounded and conservative. Because they thrive on structure, they approach most situations with that same mindset, which includes matters within the family. They tend to carefully plan ideas out before enacting them. These steady individuals are usually the family members who you know you can go to for help. They're typically willing to share their advice and wisdom with you. On the other hand, they can be fairly stubborn. If you disagree with them, it can be nearly impossible to convince them to change their mind. Once they are set on their ideals and beliefs, they rarely ever waver. They tend to be genuinely caring, but they sometimes struggle to express it clearly.

Air signs tend to be the spontaneous and open-minded members of your family. They probably don't like any restrictions that the family has implemented, as they prefer having the freedom to choose. They tend to be outgoing and friendly. When it comes to family gatherings, you can usually count on them to show up, as they'll be happy to socialize and visit. But don't depend on them to be the ones planning or running things behind the scenes. It won't happen. Air signs also tend to be the mediators within the family, able to diffuse tense situations and divert everyone back toward a more positive and relaxed exchange.

The water signs are the more emotional and heartfelt ones, often default to how they're feeling rather than relying on logic. Oftentimes, they will be the ones who will put the needs of their family above their own. Their intuition is almost scary good, and they are typically able to pick up on any tensions or conflicts within the family. So, they tend to be a good person to lean on when you are going through something. However, they can become very upset if their needs aren't looked after. If other signs do not always take notice when something is wrong, they will take it very personally. They can also hold a grudge for a very long time.

Astrological Friendship

Much like romantic and familial relationships, the zodiac can influence the friendships you make throughout your life. Some signs tend to be more compatible, as they can either balance each other out or strengthen one another.

If you're a fire sign, befriending your fellow fire signs will keep your fire going and adventurous spirit running free. Aside from that, if you're an Aries, you should also get some Gemini friends. They will fuel your desire for fun and provide you with gossip. Leos should find an Aquarians to befriend. Their spontaneous nature will keep you constantly entertained. And if you're a Sagittarius, you should befriend some Libras. They will be willing to join you in whatever adventures you plan, which is the kind of friend you need.

If you're an earth sign, then look to your fellow earth signs for the stable, grounded people you prefer to be around. Tauruses should also consider befriending some Libras. You can bond over aesthetic and material things, making them someone you can share your tastes with. If you're a Virgo, you should find a Scorpio to befriend. They can help balance you out when you are overthinking, offering you advice. Capricorns could also befriend Scorpios. They will support and respect your ambitions directly, as you need.

The flowy air signs will understand the unpredictable and free-loving nature each other has. Aside from that, you should find a Leo friend. For a Gemini, they can help give you more direction and be a positive influence. Their bright and vibrant nature can pull Libras in and match your desire to be seen. They can also influence Aquarians to keep their mental and physical health in check.

If you're a water sign, you'll find that you can connect to other water signs more deeply as you share an intuitive nature. Cancers could do with befriending some Capricorns. You can get easily overwhelmed with emotion and their focused nature can help put your mind on the right track. Frankly, Scorpios should befriend other Scorpios. No one else will get you the way that other Scorpios do. A Pisces should befriend some Virgos, as their more practical nature can help you solidify your big, dreamy ideas.

The 12 Zodiac Signs

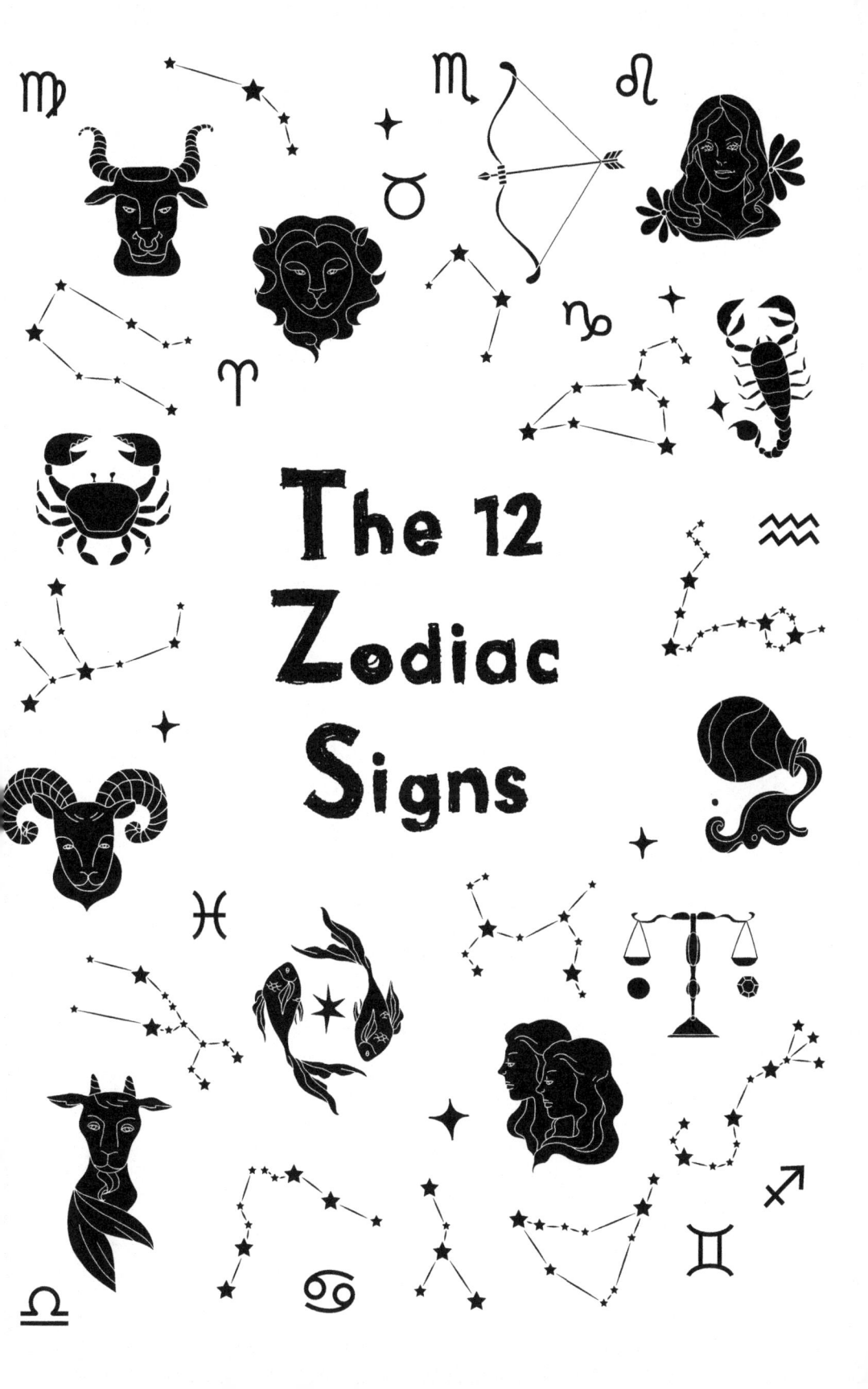

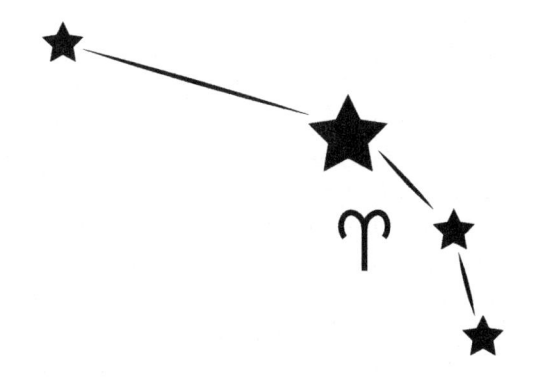

Aries

Symbol: The ram
Dates: March 20 – April 19
Element: Fire
Modality: Cardinal
Ruling planet: Mars

Aries traits
No filter
Gets angry, then forgets why they were angry
Thinks everything is a game they can win
Will do anything on a dare
Easily bored

Love

Aries has a habit of falling in love rather quickly. You don't like wasting your time and energy on things, and as such, tend to believe that you know immediately whether you have met your match or not. You will get to know people, but not necessarily for an extended period. You make your mind up about relationships quickly. But you will also end things just as quickly if you don't believe it will work out. You tend to show how you're feeling physically. On your good days, you are loving and attentive. But when you're in a bad mood, you can become hostile, pushing your loved ones away. You can end up hurting your partners without realizing it, and may sometimes need to learn how to compromise about things instead of demanding to have them your way.

Handling a Breakup

If you see signs that your relationship may be nearing an end, you will likely be the one to end it before your partner can. And to show that it was the right decision, you may even find yourself moving on quickly before your ex gets a chance to. But in doing so, you may come to realize that you regret the decision, having acted a bit rashly. An Aries may perform huge, romantic gestures to win back their exes and make amends once they realize they made a mistake. If you find yourself chasing after an ex, make sure to stop and ask yourself if you're doing it because you genuinely want to be with them again or simply because you're searching for that feeling of winning.

You may leave relationships fast, but if you're the one left, it can anger you to no end. Aries is a proud sign, full of self-love and confidence. And being broken up with can damage your ego and self-image. After all, how could someone leave you? You're the total package! Plus, you probably hate losing, and being broken up with is considered a big loss in your books. You may find that you have a hard time moving on from a breakup, despite knowing that they're the ones missing out. The problem is that you're independent enough to take your time before committing to a relationship. So, when you have invested time and energy into something, you are far less willing to move on past it without trying to make it work however you can. While this isn't necessarily a bad thing, it can be a dangerous trait, especially if you find yourself attached to someone who is simply stringing you along or is unhealthy for you.

The best way for an Aries to move on from a breakup is distance. Limit the places you see them. Block them online, get rid of their things, and try to avoid bumping into them in person if you can. Giving yourself the space and time to move on will help you to be ready for your next potential relationship.

Texting Back

You tend to be someone who texts back, but usually only if you're already on your phone. You likely prefer to keep your messages short and directly to the point. You likely don't see the need to add fluff or wordiness when you can just give a simple answer instead. If you get distracted or start to lose interest in the conversation, you'll likely stop replying quickly, or even at all.

Choosing a Career

As an Aries, you tend to be driven and competitive, making you naturally inclined to be skilled at sports. Alternatively, you may find yourself desiring a job that would make you feel a sense of self-satisfaction. You want to feel like what you're doing is important and making a difference in the world. In that case, a job like a police officer or firefighter would fit that desire, or perhaps even working within the medical field. You have natural leadership skills and you would likely make a good fit for a managerial position. You are one to tackle any challenge head-on and are not someone who will give up when things get tough. Your dedication and passion cause people to look up to you, making you flourish in this sort of position. Just let your skills and natural dedication speak for you and you will prosper. Try to avoid a desk job or a job that would force you to stay in one place. These kinds of jobs will feel too tedious, and you don't have the patience to sit still and wait for long periods.

Choosing a Major

If you're an Aries, you likely thrive in the spotlight and work hard to gain the attention and adoration of others. A great major choice for you would be the performing arts. You would glow on stage and get the attention you crave. Alternatively, you could go for a degree in business. Not only would your intelligence and creativity shine through, but getting this degree could set you up for independent success. You could become an entrepreneur and start your own business, allowing you to shape your schedule and future per your needs and wants. Or, perhaps a degree in communications is more your thing. After all, you are naturally good at communicating and networking. Plus a job in this field could keep you from being stuck in an office and give you more flexibility.

Study Tips

You tend to prefer studying alone, especially because you love learning new things. So, if something has your interest, you will likely spend plenty of time researching it. The important thing is to keep yourself motivated. This doesn't usually become an issue when the topic is interesting to you, but not everything will necessarily hold your attention the same way. Make sure to take breaks so that you can keep focused on the topic you're meant to be studying.

Attracting Wealth

As an Aries, the best way to attract money is to embrace a more practical approach to it. You shouldn't rely on any sort of get-rich-quick schemes and expect to walk away with wealth. Instead, dedicate your time and effort to more steady and dependable ways of earning money. These methods will benefit you far more in the long run. Also, you should ensure that you aren't relying on the success and support of others when it comes to financial success. Instead, be more independent in your pursuits. Financial independence will bring you an abundant amount of wealth.

Winning an Argument

Aries tend to get fired up easily, so the best way to beat them is to stay calm. Don't let them get you worked up. They tend to speak before they think when in an argument, so you'll have to remain steady and pay attention. If you can point out the flaws in what they're saying, then their argument will start to crumble.

Dealing with Stress

Whenever you get stressed, it tends to manifest itself in more physical ways. You may bite your nails, shake your leg, or something along those lines to try to express the jittery feeling. You may also be prone to pretty severe tension headaches, which don't tend to go away with a bit of rest and medicine. As an Aries, you are likely to be a private person, which includes handling a heavy amount of stress. You don't want to ruin your image as someone steady and in control. And to handle it, you may find yourself trying to overcompensate by drowning yourself in physical self-care or pushing yourself to work the stress out through exercise. But these methods won't ease the turmoil in your soul. You need a balance, and if you focus too much on your body, your mind will suffer. Try to add some meditation or yoga into the mix. These can bring a sense of inner peace and keeping both your mind and body in their top form will prepare you to handle whatever stress is weighing on you.

Boosting Your Confidence

You are a natural leader and tend to be a bright and passionate person. However, while this is a good trait, it can bubble out of control if you aren't careful. You may end up lashing out or your impatience could get the better of you, which doesn't tend to make you feel pleasant after the fact. To recover, and possibly avoid those instances in the future, try something new. Experiencing a fresh, new challenge can bring a great boost to your self-esteem. Taking on something new within your job or school can also bring more confidence, especially if you're able to satisfy your competitive side.

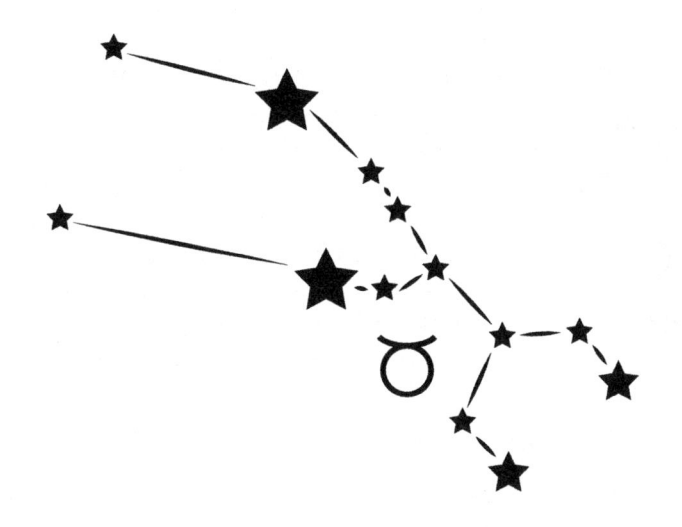

Taurus

Symbol: The Bull
Dates: April 19 – May 20
Element: Earth
Modality: Fixed
Ruling planet: Venus

TAURUS TRAITS
Just wants to cuddle
Homebody
All or nothing, no in between
Wears the same outfit everyday
Hates big changes

Love

You don't tend to fall in love quickly, and often make slow progress in a relationship until you know for sure that it's right. You trust your intuition and rely on it when settling into a long-term partnership. When you are committed, you will remain steady and serious about your partner. As a Taurus, you tend to express love in other ways, rather than just verbally. You can sometimes struggle to express how you're feeling, coming off as cold and uncaring. But that doesn't mean you're trying to hide how you feel. You just show it less directly.

Handling a Breakup

As a very stubborn sign, a Taurus may find themselves fighting for a relationship, even if it's clear that there is no saving it. If you find yourself in a failing relationship that you are struggling and fighting to keep going, it may be in your best interest to make yourself let go. If you're the one initiating the breakup, no pleading, reasoning, or outside voices will likely deter you. Your mind is made up, and your decision is unwavering. If you find out that your partner has been lying or was unfaithful, you'll likely be enraged by that betrayal and a quick breakup is sure to follow.

You don't like change, and a breakup is a massive change you would be forced to face. A Taurus considers every relationship they have as an investment, and they fully intend on building it to stand the test of time. A breakup is something you don't usually plan on. You tend to view anyone you date as a potential spouse or long-term partner. So, a breakup can surprise you and completely throw you off. You may find yourself becoming bitter and frustrated, and even growing angry and resentful due to all the time and energy you now view as wasted. This can even cause you to become defensive and push away new, potential partners.

So, what's the best way for a Taurus to get over their breakup? Ironically, it's actually to change up your routine. This, naturally, begins with cutting out the things you used to do with your ex. Continuing that routine will only upset and anger you more, keeping you from getting over them. Try going to new restaurants, coffee shops, and parks. Explore places around you and you may even find some new favorites to work into your new and improved routine. Maybe rearrange your room, pick up a new hobby—anything new! Changing your usual will help to work on the habits and things you shared with your ex until you're able to establish your new routine without them.

Texting Back

You're usually not very quick to reply to texts and instead try to take as much time as you can, especially if the person you're texting is expecting you to respond right away. You have other things you're doing, and giving them your undivided attention isn't often one of them. If you get around to answering, you likely don't worry about apologizing either. At least you answered, right?

Choosing a Career

As a Taurus, you prefer stability, consistency, and organization. You are fine with monotony and mundane tasks, so you may find a kind of enjoyment in an office job. This kind of career would keep you on a very consistent schedule, and allow you to be thorough, dedicated, and focused. That doesn't mean that your schedule will never be thrown off. After all, coworkers will come and go, meetings will be scheduled and moved, and things will change with time. Just remember to take a breath and focus on what you can do to return to that grounded and stable state of mind that you thrive in. You also tend to be a material person who enjoys pretty and aesthetically pleasing things. As such, a dull environment will take its toll on you. You will need a job that allows you to put your personal touch on things, such as an office space that you can make your own through decoration and color-coded files. Or you could consider looking for a job within the arts that will allow you not only to be around creative-minded people, but to express your creative side.

Choosing a Major

Your dedicated and focused nature and your skills with money and finances would perfectly fit pursuing a degree in finance. This would give you the kind of structure and schedule that you thrive in. If you're more of a creatively-minded Taurus, perhaps a degree in interior design would fit you a bit better. You have a natural eye for beauty and aesthetics and would likely enjoy sharing this love for beauty with others. Or you could opt for a degree in psychology. You have a particular way of viewing things, and your determination to finish whatever you dedicate yourself to is an excellent trait for this field.

Study Tips

You are a very structured person, so you prefer having a set study time. And because of that, you tend to finish your studying and work within that time frame. You usually have a pretty full schedule because of your interest in extracurriculars and other activities, so having a plan becomes even more important to keep everything in line and ensure that nothing gets missed. When it comes to studying, you should find a nice quiet place to set up to keep you focused on your work.

Attracting Wealth

For a Taurus, you should try to have a few different avenues of income to prosper. Using your different skills and crafts to find unique ways to make money will lead you down the best path to success. The idea of your income being so unstable may worry you, but you can find ways to ground it in success. Approach this concept with schedules and plans so that you can keep a sense of consistency while still being able to experiment with ways of making money. This unique approach will help you to feel accomplished and successful.

Winning an Argument

Tauruses tend to stay calm and think through their arguments before they speak. As such, the best way to get to them is to match their energy. You can also take advantage of the fact that they can get frustrated easily. Try to point out flaws in their arguments before letting them backtrack and defend themselves. Keep doing this until they can't find an argument anymore. You'll have won.

Dealing with Stress

You much prefer to handle things at a very steady pace, and when you feel pressured or forced to hurry, you can quickly get overwhelmed. You may even find yourself taking days off whenever you're under heavy stress in an attempt to recover. Somehow you've convinced yourself that things will be easier to handle after a night of rest. If you're feeling overwhelmed, you may seek out distractions to get your mind off things. Usually, this means hunkering down at home and binging that new show you've been dying to watch or pouring hours into that video game you haven't been able to keep up with. A better way to handle your stress is to introduce something new to your routine. Maybe start waking up a little earlier to go on morning walks, or pick up a hobby that you haven't been able to try out. Don't take on new things that will fill up your schedule, but rather, find things that will help ground you and remind you that you are in control.

Boosting Your Confidence

You tend to come off as someone who has everything together and doesn't need to work on their self-esteem, but that's not always the case deep down. If you're feeling a bit down on yourself, take a moment to step back and look at all you have accomplished. You should be proud of your achievements, big and small. You're also someone who enjoys and appreciates your material things, so taking the time to appreciate them and the success that they symbolize will help to lift your self-esteem. You're a sturdy and hardy person. You have incredible mental strength and have overcome plenty of things in the past. You can handle a lot more than you may sometimes give yourself credit for, that's for sure.

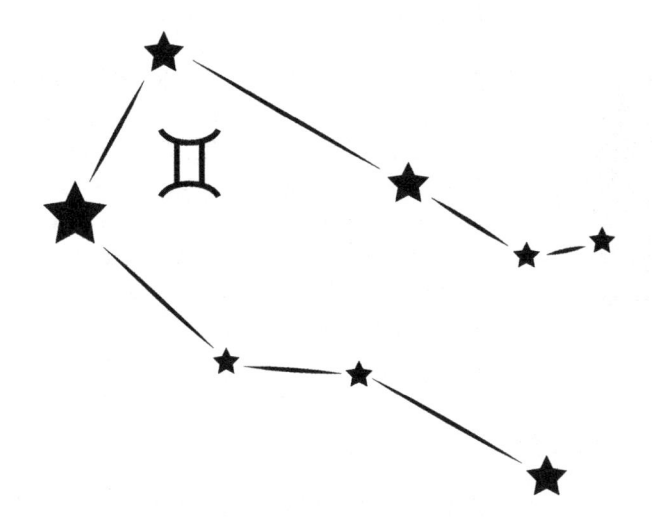

Gemini

Symbol: The Twins
Dates: May 20 – June 21
Element: Air
Modality: Mutable
Ruling planet: Mercury

Gemini traits
Charismatic
Uses humor as a crutch
Could talk to a brick wall
Arguments as flirting
Knows a little about everything

Love

Geminis can fall in love fast and hard. You are infatuated with new and unique people. It can be pretty easy for someone to flirt their way into your life, but that doesn't mean they'll become a permanent fixture. Your curiosity makes you unpredictable in relationships because, just as quickly as you fall in love, you can fall out of it. You are usually interested in relationships for fun and aren't keen on being with a permanent partner. It's not uncommon for Geminis to be in a new relationship every couple of weeks.

Handling a Breakup

There are two sides to a Gemini, which is made abundantly clear when they're going through a breakup. You tend to rely on open communication, and that parallels your relationships. Just as you may speak every day when you're interested in someone, when it's over, you'll cut all lines. You're also probably known for ghosting people you lose interest in. After all, it's better than having to confront them directly. If you decide to break up with your partner, you likely twist things so that they feel like they're the ones making the decision rather than you. This may seem a bit manipulative to some, as Geminis use these tactics to avoid unnecessary conflict while also coming out looking like the good guy and still getting what they want in the end.

If you're broken up with, your first reaction is likely to overanalyze everything. You likely run yourself ragged trying to evaluate and go over everything you could have done wrong, what you could have done differently, or where things went awry. This will only lead you to mental and emotional exhaustion if you keep it going. Remember to fall back onto the logical part of yourself. You can't evaluate every possibility, and you're only wearing yourself down. However, you will also be quick to save face and show everyone around you (including your ex) that you're totally fine without them. You will likely immediately want to go out with friends and do things to get your mind off of your ex. You may even find yourself telling all your friends and posting online about how fine you are, that the breakup was for the best, and making it seem like you don't care that it's over.

Remember that it's important for you to acknowledge the emotions you're trying to avoid. While moving on quickly may seem like a win, if you're completely dodging how you feel, you'll never healthily get over your ex. By all means, distract yourself. But don't be afraid to feel upset and angry. Cry, vent, scream, and do what you have to do to let those feelings go. As a Gemini, one of the best ways for you to get your feelings out is to talk about them. Vent to your friends or even write things down. If you don't get those feelings out, you may become bitter. Or you might carry around resentment that could damage your future potential relationships.

Texting Back

Sometimes, a conversation will strike your fancy, or you may even just feel extra talkative. On those days, you can talk endlessly. You'll be quick to answer texts and even give elaborate replies when you're on a roll. But you tend to have a lot on your mind. As such, if you're not feeling it, you can easily lose interest in the conversation or even skip replying entirely.

Choosing a Career

You excel at conversation and have an innate desire to express yourself. As such, many Geminis make wonderful songwriters, novelists, poets, and playwrights. These careers would allow you to express your creative side while sharing your thoughts with the world. Alternatively, you may be fit for a job in journalism. Your curious nature and desire to explore would be met, and your communication abilities would help you excel in this field. No matter what kind of job you decide to pursue, it's important to avoid one with a very rigid and set schedule. A constant routine will only frustrate you, and you need a job that allows you to be flexible and make your schedule. It's very possible to find a career like this, or perhaps you should consider self-employment or freelance work instead. These options would allow you to make your schedule and change it however you please, while still pursuing the kind of jobs you wish to take. You are independent by nature, so having a job that allows you to be your own boss is another bonus.

Choosing a Major

Your curiosity and desire to explore and be out in the world would be a great fit for a major in journalism. Plus the flexibility of it will benefit you. Besides, you're excellent at communication. In a similar vein, perhaps a marketing major would be a good fit. Your creative mind could help any business you work for to flourish. If you're more interested in expressing yourself creatively, a performing arts major is another good idea. Not only can you express yourself and interact with other people, but you will also have the ability to move from one project to the next. You won't be tied down to a specific, rigid schedule and the same dull place.

Study Tips

Your natural intelligence and ability to remember even small details make it easy for you to study. However, you may find studying a bit boring and unenjoyable, and it can lose your focus and cause your grades to suffer. Thanks to your social nature, perhaps you should try studying with friends. Being able to share ideas and points of view will not only keep you interested in what you're studying, but it could also help you expand your perspective and mind.

Attracting Wealth

You should approach your finances with the understanding that they will fluctuate. Expect things to shift and prepare so that it doesn't throw you for a loop. Make sure you have money saved just in case those moments come. You're very financially minded, so follow this intuition when planning for monetary pursuits. Trust your gut. If you ever feel that you are struggling financially, you should take a step back and focus on what may be distressing you emotionally. Once you are more balanced, you will notice that the money-making ease will return.

Winning an Argument

They sure can talk up a storm whenever they're in an argument, but Geminis also tend to avoid details. Just because they can talk, doesn't mean they're right. So you'll have to remain calm and quiet and wait for them to forget a detail or gloss over a point. You'll be able to catch them and completely dismantle their argument.

Dealing with Stress

To put it rather bluntly, you don't deal with your stress. Instead, you internalize it and try to bury and ignore it. But this causes the feelings to worsen and fester, which often leads to an outburst or pushes you to lash out. The stress may manifest in nervous energy, causing you to pace about your house or throw yourself into a specific project. A better way to handle your stress is to find ways to calm yourself and allow yourself to unwind healthily. Maybe try to find some calming playlists to listen to. Or you can invite a friend who can help you process your feelings and sort out your stress so it's not consuming you. They could also help clear your mind by watching a movie or playing a game with you. Something cathartic and refreshing is the best way to go.

Boosting Your Confidence

As an intellectual, you tend to lose confidence when faced with something that you aren't familiar with. You may feel the need to convey exactly how you're feeling, but this can sometimes backfire, depending on the situation and how those around you take it. The best way for you to gain confidence is to take the role of the leader. Taking the reins of a project or an event can do wonders for your self-esteem. Also, try discussing things with your friends and acquaintances. If you can steer the conversation toward topics you know, you'll feel a confidence boost. You enjoy getting to share your knowledge over a good and intelligent conversation, so use it to your advantage.

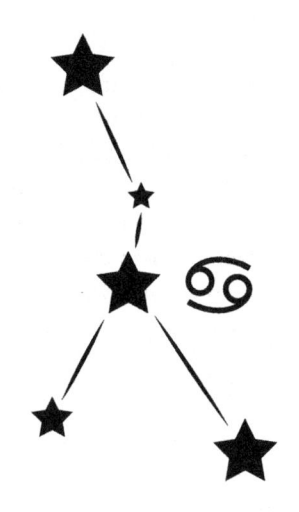

Cancer

Symbol: The crab
Dates: June 21 – July 22
Element: Water
Modality: Cardinal
Ruling planet: The Moon

CANCER TRAITS
Very sensitive
Seeks comfort
Forgives but never forgets
Only has one boundary, but it is very firm
Takes on other people's problems

Love

While you may appear more reserved, you are romantic at your core and tend to fall in love rather quickly. But you have a habit of falling in love with an idealistic version of your partner and the relationship you want, rather than the person themself. While you crave affection and intimacy, you also fear it is coming from an untrustworthy place. As such, you struggle to love someone who loves you. If you can manage to love your partner rather than your ideal of love, you can overflow with emotion. You will likely carry love for them for the rest of your life.

Handling a Breakup

Cancers are very protective of their hearts, and as such, it takes them a long time to trust someone enough to enter a relationship with them. But when they do have one, they don't want to lose it, and they will fight to keep it going. Turning their ex into a villain is the route they go to protect themselves. Doing so separates you from them, and is the easiest way for you to put space between you and the cause of your heartache. You may even set boundaries for yourself to further protect your broken heart. The support of your friends will be your biggest asset during this time.

As a Cancer, you tend to avoid short-term relationships, and instead, often latch onto a romantic partner who shows potential in being more long term. And when they end, you have a habit of taking them hard. When you find yourself at the receiving end of a breakup, your initial reaction is typically to defame your ex to everyone around. But this is just a front to further protect yourself, and behind the scenes, you may isolate yourself or confide in your closest friends. Cancers also tend to cling to reminders of their ex as they heal.

As you're getting over your breakup, you may find yourself avoiding any potential, new romance. You may be scared to trust again and to be hurt again, so instead, you harden your shell and avoid it altogether. But this is far from a healthy way of handling it. After all, avoiding any love also keeps you from experiencing the good parts of relationships. Instead, you should focus on mending your heart. Let go of physical reminders of your ex so that those memories can start to fade. Spend time around friends who help you heal, rather than just using them as a distraction.

Texting Back

If you receive texts that are confrontational or aggressive, you will avoid replying for as long as you can. You are sensitive to this kind of energy, and as such, you don't want to bring more of it in by giving them an answer. But if it's a message from someone you love, then it's a different story. You'll try to reply as quickly as you can. If you can't answer fast enough, you'll start feeling guilty.

Choosing a Career

Your high level of sensitivity also means that you care a lot about the people around you. You likely dedicate a lot of time to making sure your friends are taking care of themselves, even spending days finding them the perfect birthday present or making sure they get their homework done. As such, the perfect kind of career for you would be one where you can help others. You won't enjoy a job that makes you feel like you aren't making a sort of impact on the lives of others. Jobs in education or childcare are some options, but that doesn't mean they are the only ones that can make you feel satisfied. You could even pursue more creative careers or entrepreneur opportunities. You tend to be sensitive whenever you're criticized, so you should seek out jobs filled with positive reinforcement. Those are the kinds of places where you would thrive. You need a job that offers you a level of support that is similar to what you give out. Otherwise, you're more likely to lose your motivation for the work you do.

Choosing a Major

Your kind and caring nature, and your desire to help others, would make you the perfect candidate for a degree in education. Or you can go for pre-med instead, which will allow you to nurture and take care of people. Both of these degrees would put you in a position to feel as though you're making a positive impact, which will leave you feeling happy and fulfilled. If neither of those fit you, maybe you can opt for a degree in hospitality and tourism. You would still be helping people, even if it's not in the most conventional way.

Study Tips

You always get your best studying done when you are in an emotionally happy place. If you feel off, you may find it difficult to focus on your work. An observer by nature, you try to learn things and relate them to what you witness for yourself. A great way to do this is to converse with friends after studying. This can help you to retain and understand it even better. If you get stuck, you should try to come up with new studying methods to help get you out of your funk. Just remember that you work best in a place where you are comfortable, especially when you have a big workload.

Attracting Wealth

You should approach money and your pursuits of wealth with a high level of integrity. If you are not making morally sound decisions when pursuing money, it will not be a consistent and steady income for you. Stay constant in your efforts and have enough confidence to not give up if things get a bit complicated. Taking the initiative will generate success. Also, be generous! Generosity with your money will only attract more wealth.

Winning an Argument

Cancers are driven by emotion, and that includes arguments. As such, they can sometimes come off as manipulative when trying to get you to see their point of view. You have to make sure to stick to your argument and not let them sway you. Stubbornly refuse to budge and they'll lose the ability to argue with you.

Dealing with Stress

Stress can take a heavy toll on you, and you have a habit of simply hiding away whenever you get overwhelmed. As a Cancer, you can be fairly sensitive to things and may default to seeking out pity from others whenever you're having a particularly rough time. Something to remember is that it would do you some good to spend a bit of time alone with your thoughts. Take time to have space for yourself and process your feelings without relying on others. Maybe pour your thoughts out into a written form or even a recording. Letting out your true and honest feelings will help you understand yourself better. They can also make you realize what you need to get back on the right path. Alternatively, you can spend your time doing something productive and fun, like expressing yourself creatively or getting into a hobby. Not only can it keep you from wallowing in your thoughts, but it can also feel rewarding. There is a balance to it though, so make sure you aren't depending too heavily on your alone time or you may become defensive toward those who care about you.

Boosting Your Confidence

You tend to lack confidence in yourself and may struggle to find ways to boost it. There are a few practices you should consider picking up when trying to give a lift to your self-esteem. You tend to value the opinions of those close to you, so surround yourself with the people you love. Just being around them can bring a surge of confidence to a weary Cancer. You are the kind of person who is always looking out for your friends. Remember that they know that they can rely on you and that you've probably helped them through some difficult times. They probably consider themselves lucky to have you in their lives. Don't forget that.

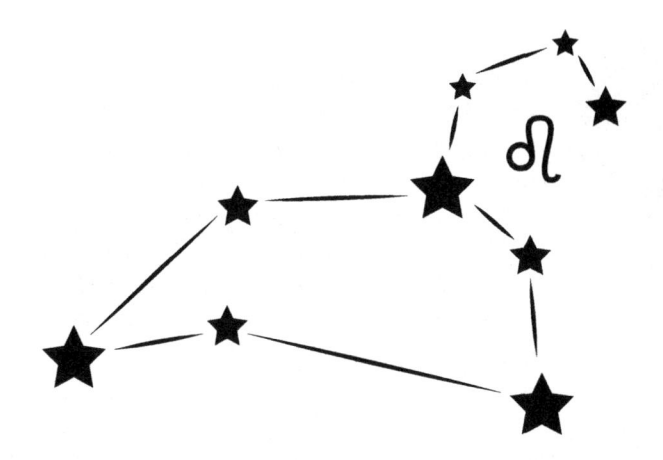

Leo

Symbol: The Lion
Dates: July 22 – August 22
Element: Fire
Modality: Fixed
Ruling planet: The Sun

Leo traits
Exudes warmth and creativity
A little bit vain
Really big personality
Wants to stand out
Interested in luxury

Love

You want a partner who can match you step by step. You are energetic and showy, and you want to be with someone who has just as much confidence. You are drawn to intellectual people. You want to hold a long conversation while also enjoying how your partner eloquently speaks. Leos may enjoy the spotlight, but oftentimes, you use this as a sort of defense mechanism. You can be quite insecure deep down. As such, you can be drawn to partners who are more spontaneous and chaotic than you are. You seek the balance that they can bring to the relationship.

Handling a Breakup

Leos are passionate and extravagant, which naturally bleeds into all aspects of romance. You are likely enchanted easily by romance and tend to fall for infatuation very quickly. If you are ever the one to initiate the split yourself, you are likely over that relationship pretty quickly. After all, it was on your terms. But when broken up with, you likely feel an extreme amount of pain and anguish over the ended relationship. Others may see your emotional reaction as dramatic and over the top, but it feels more than reasonable to you. During these times, it's best to look to your close friends for comfort and help in healing.

You're a hopeless romantic, and as such, you may often do whatever you can to keep your relationship together. You may even be willing to forgive behaviors and acts worthy of a breakup just to stay with them. And you'll make sure no one on the outside has any idea what's going on behind the scenes. With how public your relationships are, the breakups are often bordering on the all-out theatrical. You may even be the kind of person who constantly breaks up and makes up with your partner, much to the frustration of your friends.

One of the best ways for a Leo to heal after a broken heart is to express yourself creatively. Whatever art forms you enjoy, venting your emotions through them can be calming and therapeutic. Not only will it help to get those emotions out, but it will also get you back to feeling like your normal self. No matter how low you may feel when you have reached this moment, always remember that you will find yourself again. You're a lion, after all.

Texting Back

You'll be fast to respond to positive and enjoyable text messages, even if they are just emoji spam between you and your friends. But the moment that a conversation veers onto a boring topic, you'll lose interest and fast. Annoying messages, or even critical ones, are just not interesting to you. You'll often take as long as you like to reply to those—if you even decide to.

Choosing a Career

Thanks to your big personality and radiance, it's no surprise when people suggest you take up a career that puts you in the spotlight. Anything from politics to television, Leos tend to thrive in roles that get them the level of attention they crave. Despite that, you have a fragile side, and if you are particularly easily upset, you may want to reevaluate your desire to be in the public eye. Either that or learn how to ignore hurtful words from strangers. You will likely seek a job that helps support your ideals and beliefs, and despite being a bit of a show-off, you have a pure heart and good intentions. As such, having a job that also gives you an ability to help others will satisfy that desire. Whether it's donating time and money to charitable causes or passing laws to help societal issues, making a difference is important to you. To top it all off, you have a strong sense of loyalty. You are very dependable and work well in a team setting, so you will flourish in a career that allows you to work with others instead of being entirely independent.

Choosing a Major

Naturally, one of the best majors for you to pick would be political science. You have the leadership skills that could put you in the political office one day. Or perhaps a degree in performing arts would fit you a bit better. A personality as loud and bright as yours would do well on a stage or a television screen. If you're a Leo who isn't too keen on being in the spotlight, maybe a degree in education is for you. You'll still have the attention of others while being able to fulfill your desire to make a difference.

Study Tips

You would prefer to avoid studying if you can, and are only really interested in it when it's about something that you want to learn. Your confidence tends to get the better of you in these situations and you may assume that you know more than you do. One way to keep your focus on studying is to make note of key details or words. Doing so will help you learn and retain the information better. You could also find ways to motivate yourself to finish your studies.

Attracting Wealth

You should take a more organized and practical approach to making money. Pay close attention to every detail. Allowing things to go unchecked can cause your profits to suffer.

Have an established plan and budget that you stick to. You also want to make sure that you only make your money through your efforts, not through underhanded means. If not, it will only blow up in your face. Managing your resources will bring a more abundant income. Also, spending your wealth on only fun and extravagant things for yourself will not bring the consistent income you are working toward.

Winning an Argument

Leos can get heated quickly, and have a knack for thinking up arguments instantly. But they can also run out of steam pretty fast. Don't let them work you up, because you'll never win that argument. Instead, ask them questions and keep them going. The more you can get them to talk, the quicker they'll lose interest in the argument.

Dealing with Stress

Whenever you get stressed, you tend to put on a brave face until you're alone, and then you may find yourself just breaking down and crying. And typically, after that strong emotional burst, you tend to feel much better. You can rationalize your stress and put it into a new perspective, and may even find humor in the situation you're in. You tend to thrive under pressure, as you like proving to everyone that you can handle whatever is thrown at you. Stress just adds another layer to that. You have a habit of taking too much on your plate and refusing to admit that you need help. Working well in those situations doesn't negate your stress, and it can manifest itself in physical ways, even causing you to feel physically ill. You may find that you isolate yourself when you're feeling overwhelmed, but the best way to combat your stress is to do the opposite. Try to cut back on some of your work where you can and instead, go out with friends. Being able to let go and enjoy socializing will help you release some of that feeling and enjoy the moment. And when you get back to work, you'll feel refreshed.

Boosting Your Confidence

You're pretty confident in yourself, and for the most part, your confidence doesn't tend to take a hit. You probably prefer to be at the center of attention, and when you are, your self-esteem tends to be at an all-time high. Just keep in mind that not everyone is going to like you. Don't let the opinions of a handful of people cause your confidence to suffer. You'll never be able to please everyone, as it's impossible. Focus instead on your own goals and the plans that you have established. Accomplishing what your heart is set on will give you the biggest boost of confidence.

Virgo

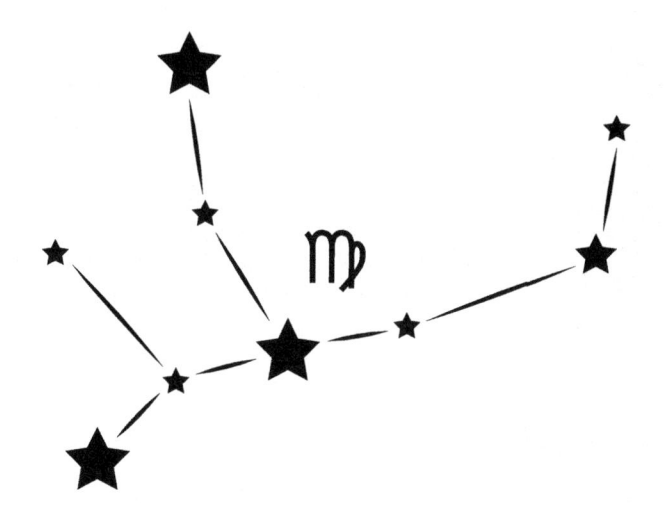

Symbol: The Virgin
Dates: August 22 – September 22
Element: Earth
Modality: Mutable
Ruling planet: Mercury

Virgo traits
Needs to feel useful
Has a quick fix for everything
Judgmental, but with good intentions
Exceptional spatial awareness
A million ideas per second

Love

Virgos don't tend to favor love or romance. Often you view love as an impractical and impossible thing. You may even believe that what you're looking for doesn't even exist on the same plane as you do. You are reaching for something entirely unobtainable. You prefer to be in control as much as possible, and something like romance is highly emotional and the exact opposite of control. But it's far from impossible for you to find love. And when you do, it can be an incredible feeling.

Handling a Breakup

Your analytical mindset tends to make you a bit of a perfectionist, including in relationships. You tend to have very high expectations, many of which are fairly unrealistic. If this ideal that you have isn't met, you may have a habit of starting to doubt your relationship, and even already deciding it won't work before the breakup even happens. Virgos don't like conflict, so if you're trying to initiate a breakup, you prefer to take full responsibility so that the other person doesn't feel hurt. You may feel guilty after the fact, potentially finding yourself still helping your ex in some manner, whether it be emotionally or financially.

After a breakup, a Virgo will often question what happened. You'll likely end up analyzing any and every possible thing that you can. What if you did this differently? What if you never said that? Would it have worked out if this didn't happen? You will have to stop and force yourself to quit focusing so much on the "what-ifs," or else you will only make yourself feel worse. Distractions are often the best way to do this as they can keep your mind and hands busy for a while. If you aren't dwelling in remorse, you may instead find yourself attacking your ex. You will find anything wrong with them and will blame your breakup on all their negative qualities, even if those were things you would have defended when you were together.

You are a perfectionist, and as such, you seek perfection in your relationships. This causes you to be defensive after a breakup to avoid getting your heart broken again. You may find yourself seeking any relationship advice that you can get your hands on. Self-help books, blogs, videos online—whatever can help you avoid what happened last time is all fair game! On the other hand, you may instead focus on your friends, neglecting your feelings and helping them with their problems. But remember that you shouldn't let your feelings sit and fester without processing them. Talking them over does wonders for healing wounds. No relationship is perfect, so don't push potential partners away by worrying over tiny flaws and past heartaches. Take your time to heal, but don't be afraid to try again.

Texting Back

If you're texting someone who is receptive and appreciative of your time and effort, you'll likely send rather long and elaborate messages, especially if that friend can keep up with your flow. If you don't have the time, you still try to make some sort of response to messages. Letting texts go unanswered will only leave you stressed.

Choosing a Career

As a neat and very detail-focused Virgo, you would naturally fit into careers that require a level of focus and organization. Data collection, scientific fields, or finance-based careers are all ones that fall into that category. But that doesn't mean those are the only kinds of jobs that would suit you. Your skills could flourish in all sorts of careers, even those in creative fields. You tend to prefer working conditions to remain professional, so you'll want a job where you can avoid drama or gossip among your coworkers. You tend to approach work as a background or supporting character. Rather than taking control as the leader, you typically default to just being part of the crowd. That being said, you may find that you would make a great leader. Your very specific and focused way of thinking can help lay out a clear and concise plan for your team to follow. And you may even find that you enjoy being in a leadership position. Your excellent problem-solving skills and ability to clear up even the most muddled issues are the traits that will help you in this position. You may be surprised by how many people appreciate the skills you have.

Choosing a Major

Your perfectionist nature and strict attention to detail would fit a degree in accounting. The need to be precise is within your skillset. Alternatively, you could go for a degree in criminal justice. That detail-focused mind of yours would make for an excellent detective. You could also opt for a degree in journalism. Your focus and attentiveness to research would help you flourish as a journalist. Or, you could flex the perfectionist parts of your mind as an editor.

Study Tips

You don't tend to retain the information you study when you're alone, so you should find study groups to be a part of. Talking things out with others can help you to retain information much better. You can also record lectures with your phone or look up videos that explain concepts you're struggling to grasp. Sometimes you just need someone to explain it out loud for it to click.

Attracting Wealth

You should approach wealth with a more balanced mindset. Be practical when it comes to decisions that revolve around money, and never try to rush into things. Taking the time to think over and evaluate all possibilities before deciding will bring you the greatest reward. You could also consider getting advice from a few trusted friends before settling on your decision, as they can offer new perspectives. On that note, you should also consider finding a business partner to join you in financial endeavors. Working alongside someone you trust can bring you a greater amount of success.

Winning an Argument

Virgos don't tend to start arguments, preferring to keep their opinions and thoughts to themselves. And when they do argue, it's often because they've thought of exactly what to say. Instead of focusing on what they're saying, try to look out for points they didn't mention. Forcing them to think on the spot can quickly cause them to deflate and lose interest in keeping it up.

Dealing with Stress

Due to your perfectionist nature, you have a habit of being stressed all the time. You want to handle everything yourself, and probably think that the way you do things is the only right way. If someone offers to help, you end up snapping at them. After all, their suggestion will never be as good as the method you decide on. You are intelligent, but hard on yourself, and you will often be critical of what you're doing and how you're handling things. You may even project these feelings onto others when you're particularly stressed. To combat your typical high-stress levels, you should establish a quiet and peaceful environment. This should be a place that makes you feel calm and at ease. It will balance the turmoil that you're dealing with inside. Have this kind of space set up within your home that you can hide in when you need time to focus and sort through things.

Boosting Your Confidence

You strive for absolute perfection, so when you don't meet those lofty goals, your confidence can suffer. Remember that it's important to make sure that your goals are reasonable and manageable. You're not going to be perfect, no matter how hard you try, so take the time to celebrate your accomplishments, even if they seem small. Virgos try to plan every detail, so when something doesn't work out as anticipated, it can affect you. It's okay to go out of your comfort zone! You may even find that stepping out of the confines of your meticulous planning helps to boost your confidence again.

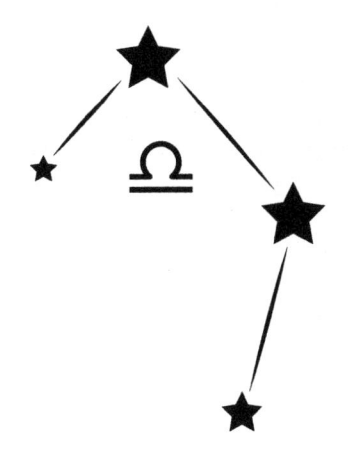

Libra

Symbol: The Scales
Dates: September 22 – October 23
Element: Air
Modality: Cardinal
Ruling planet: Venus

LIBRA TRAITS
Hates being alone
Really good aesthetics
Conflict avoidant
Sees every side
Prone to fantasy
Can't make decisions

Love

Libras are fascinated by beauty and aesthetics. But despite enjoying expressing your beauty, you are far from shallow. You can find beauty in everything, even the flaws and quirks of other people. Anyone is capable of beauty. You are drawn to people who can help you sort out the contradictions existing in your being. You need someone sturdy and reliant when you are going through rough times. You also tend to seek out partners who share your opinions and perspectives.

Handling a Breakup

You probably love romance and enjoy being in more casual relationships for a while. You're typically open to dropping someone when another potential partner catches your attention. After all, if you don't know for sure what you want, why bother settling for someone who may not satisfy your future expectations? You would probably be much happier if breakups just weren't a thing you had to worry about and you could move on without worrying over the technicalities of them. So, when you are the one to initiate the breakup, you will likely try to be less direct. You'll also ensure that the relationship ends on the best terms possible. After all, your reputation is at stake, not just feelings.

You have a habit of flirting shamelessly and experiencing a series of flings. However, serious and committed relationships are a different story. A Libra will take their time to seek out the best possible option for a long-term partner. You may feel out various potential people and weigh different possibilities before finally deciding on someone. And when you do settle for that person, you don't intend on leaving their side. You thrive on a life of balance, so when the scales are tipped due to an unexpected breakup, you can spiral into an emotional pit of sorts. This can manifest itself in a deep depressive state or irrational, abrupt decisions to try to distract yourself from the heartache.

The best way for a Libra to heal is time. To help with that healing process, you should start by removing any reminders of your ex from your environment. Your home will return to its more aesthetically pleasing feeling while keeping memories at bay. And make sure to give yourself some self-care! Bubble baths, face masks, your favorite chocolates—whatever brings you comfort and makes you feel good are useful. Not only that, but treating yourself can help you feel like yourself again.

Texting Back

You're probably fairly well known in your friend group as the person who doesn't reply to texts. Truth is, you tend to forget because of how much else you have going on. But you may have moments in which you'll be quick to answer and actively keep up the conversation. Usually, this is when the topic you're discussing holds your interest.

Choosing a Career

You're a very well-rounded person with several skills and interests, so there are many kinds of jobs that may strike your fancy. Your biggest trait, however, is your desire for balance and equality. The sense of justice that you have may cause you to pursue jobs within the judicial system, such as a lawyer or a judge. Your ability to negotiate and persuade others to a different point of view is exceptional, making you excel in a career in politics. No matter what job you decide to pursue, it should be something that you are passionate about. Once you find that niche, you will be all in, and that will bring out the best version of yourself. You'll find that people enjoy having you on their team once they realize how cooperative and dedicated you are. Whatever you set your mind to, you will put every bit of your energy into it, and ensure that it gets done right.

Choosing a Major

Naturally, one of the best potential majors for you would be pre-law. Your desire for justice and equality would cause you to flourish in any career that this degree would help you to find. You could also go for a degree in journalism due to your dedication to truth and an avoidance of biases. On the other hand, if you're more into the aesthetic balance and beauty of things, a major in architecture may fit you better.

Study Tips

You tend to have difficulty focusing and may get distracted easily from whatever studying you're trying to do. The best way to manage this is to set up a schedule for yourself. If you can break up your time into chunks of working and relaxing, you can find a balance that will keep you from getting too antsy. Just make sure you stick to the schedule you make and keep distractions out of the picture when you're trying to work.

Attracting Wealth

You should be private with your financial moves. Having money set aside and making moves discreetly will show promising results. Keep your eyes peeled for your chance to make a move. Within moments of crises or major shifts, you may find the perfect opportunity to strike. These kinds of moments can lead you to the more abundant wealth that you're looking for, so make sure to take them whenever they present themselves to you.

Winning an Argument

Libras don't want to argue. They would rather that everyone got along with one another. So, if they end up in an argument, it's likely in an attempt to get everyone to see things the same way. The best way to defeat them is to rationalize your argument as much as possible. Eventually, they'll give up, and settle for understanding your perspective, even if they don't agree.

Dealing with Stress

You don't tend to handle stress well at all. Balance is a key trait for a Libra, and if something throws you off, it can seem like a catastrophic event. And you don't tend to be the kind of person who works through their stress. Instead, you would much rather wait until you're in a better headspace before you approach something again. You tend to be reliant on other people and often go to those you trust for advice. You highly value their opinions and they can help you work out what you're feeling. When you're feeling overwhelmed, don't just shut down. Instead, try to vent out your feelings through creative arts. Write out your thoughts, express them through painting, or channel your emotions into music. The arts are important to Libras, so they're the perfect method to help relieve overwhelming stress.

Boosting Your Confidence

Your social nature can hurt your confidence in the long run if you find yourself being too focused on pleasing others. Try not to fall into the habit of comparing yourself to other people. You will only end up damaging your self-esteem. Instead, focus on all the wonderful and unique aspects of yourself. Try embracing the arts and music that speak to you. It will help to ease your soul and bring confidence back. Remember that it's impossible to make everyone happy, so try to shrug off those who seek to tear you down. Don't let their bitterness poison you.

Scorpio

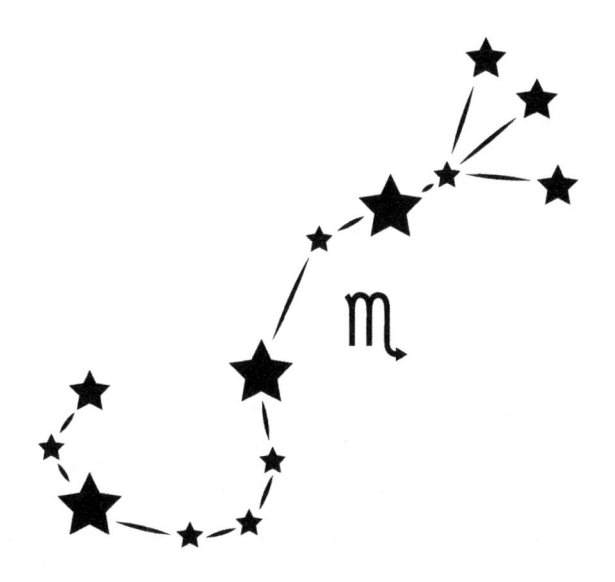

Symbol: The scorpion
Dates: October 23 – November 22
Element: Water
Modality: Fixed
Ruling planet: Pluto

Scorpio traits
Primary emotion is betrayal
Looks cool in a leather jacket
OK with uncomfortable silence
Can't be sure if they're serious or joking
Eyes that look into your soul

Love

People may find themselves falling for Scorpios easily, but they shouldn't expect you to return that feeling with any swiftness. You rarely open up enough to let love flood in. To you, love means releasing some control and setting yourself up to get hurt—both of which you would much rather avoid. If someone can manage to gain your love, you can become attached, bordering on possessive. Just as you study the people around you, you want to know everything that you possibly can about your partner.

Handling a Breakup

Scorpios tend to have a difficult time letting go in relationships, even if they are the ones who are initiating the breakup. Whether the relationship was healthy and happy or not doesn't matter to you. The thought of losing your grip on something, or someone, will cause your more controlling side to come out.

You don't tend to like getting into committed relationships, as you know that if you trust someone enough to let them in, you'll grow extremely attached. But the scariest part to you is the breakup. As a Scorpio, the emotions you tend to feel are powerful and extreme. So, you know that the heartache you would experience at the end of a relationship would be catastrophic. You may find yourself avoiding them, or even refusing to let your walls down, even for someone you do end up with. You often don't realize just how much you cared about your partner until after a breakup. After all, if any romantic feelings can survive that, then it must be true love, right? The biggest problem with your theory is that your ex-partner likely won't feel the same. While you spent so long pushing them away, protecting yourself, and keeping an iron grip on your heart, they were struggling to be allowed in to convince you to open up. Once they've given up to the point of a breakup, they're likely not willing to try again.

The best way for you to move on is to focus your attention on something else. After a breakup, you may find yourself developing obsessive behaviors. Maybe you're constantly checking your ex's socials or questioning where they are or who they're with. You need to let go of this behavior and instead focus on yourself. The only way you can truly heal from, and move past, a breakup is to acknowledge the emotions you have built up. You have to face those fears and buried feelings before you can start to recover more completely. Consider it a transformation or a new beginning.

Texting Back

You can love long, extensive conversations with certain people. These are the friends who you've had back and forth texts with for months on end. You're also the kind of person who likes to talk about deeper topics rather than just casual chatter. Despite that, you sometimes have days in which you have no interest in your phone or texting. You may leave your friends wondering what you were distracted by.

Choosing a Career

As a Scorpio, you enjoy having the attention of people. Good or bad, you don't care. You just want eyes on you, and those who want to tear you down only motivate you to try twice as hard. Just as you can be charming, you can be equally as repulsive, depending on who you ask. It's no surprise then that you would excel in a position of political power. You have a knack for persuading others and live for the thrill of a heated debate, no matter the topic. You may also thrive in any job that puts you on television, giving you the attention you crave. While you may not care much about the opinions of others, your own opinions are an entirely different matter. You have a habit of being hard on yourself and letting self-doubt plague you. This will easily bleed into your work, but don't let it stop you from pursuing the job that your heart desires. Focus on the determination that you have and let it lead you.

Choosing a Major

A degree in finance could fit you well, as you're naturally smart with money. Or you could go for a degree in pre-med. You work excellently under pressure and in a crisis, which would make you perfect for the fast-paced and stressful environment of a hospital. Another good choice would be picking a psychology major. After all, you're talented at getting people to talk and divulge things to you.

Study Tips

You're the kind of person who likes to figure things out without the input of others, so you would benefit from studying by yourself. Thanks to your hardworking nature, you don't need the motivation of others to keep you focused. You can motivate yourself just fine. You enjoy solving problems so you need to be alone to feel satisfied when getting answers.

Attracting Wealth

To bring wealth to yourself, you also have to learn to be giving with what you have. It's important to be generous and understand that there is enough for everyone in this world to live comfortable lives. Once you embrace that concept, you will begin to attract the wealth you are looking for. Don't let that stop you from continuing to give to those who need it. No matter how hard things may get, the universe will always provide the support you need.

Winning an Argument

How you handle a Scorpio can vary depending on what kind you're arguing with. If they're more old-fashioned, you can win against them easily by asking challenging questions or just outright getting on their nerves. They'll shut down pretty fast. If they're more of a modern Scorpio, start pointing out things they don't know. Poking holes in their argument with facts will cause them to fizzle out.

Dealing with Stress

You tend to let stress build up to a significant amount before you decide to deal with it. You let it simmer below the surface until you have no choice but to face those unchecked feelings. Despite being a sensitive person, you would rather hide that part of yourself from those around you, so you will retreat into yourself when you are overwhelmed. You're the kind of person who doesn't like to talk to your friends about what you have going on, but then gets upset when they don't seem to know what's stressing you out. Remember that your friends can't read your mind, and if you want them to help and support you, you will have to confide in them. Try to get a handle on your stress before it gets to be too much. It will help you to avoid being consumed by unchecked stress and anxiety. Don't be ashamed of yourself for needing the time to feel better. Just embrace how much lighter you feel after the fact.

Boosting Your Confidence

Scorpios tend to be pretty comfortable in their skin, so if you've ever been through a situation that caused your confidence to suffer, you probably knew a few ways to handle it. You will prefer to analyze the situation and decide the best way to solve it. That act in itself likely boosts your confidence, as it can remind you that you know what you're doing. Sometimes you may struggle to express what's on your mind to others. If you're looking for someone to vent to, try to find someone who can read between the lines and help guide you to the heart of the problem.

Sagittarius

Symbol: The Archer
Dates: November 22 – December
Element: Fire
Modality: Mutable
Ruling planet: Jupiter

SAGITTARIUS TRAITS
No indoor voice
Forms opinions off of pure emotion
Obsessed with self-improvement
Wields their truth like a blunt weapon
Friendliest person at the party

Love

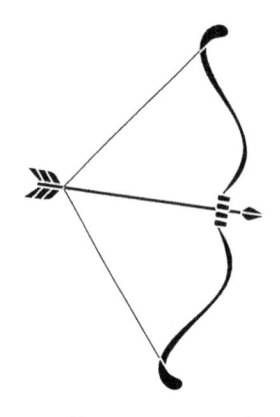

Your openness leads you to fall in love often. You don't worry about the consequences because, in your mind, you've already decided that it would be worth it. But just because you love easily doesn't mean you will stick around for an extended period. You view emotions as fluid and ever-changing, which includes love which is enjoyable, but not a necessity. On top of that, you get very restless and bored easily. You aren't keen on holding onto a relationship that may outweigh your true desire for exploration.

Handling a Breakup

You're a free spirit, and as such, aren't drawn into the idea of commitment. You're often the one leaving broken hearts in your wake. You don't like being controlled, and the first sign of a partner trying to rein in your desire for freedom can cause you to cut it off. If you're the one to break up with your partner, you tend to be very straightforward, not feeling the need to beat around the bush just to save some feelings. You are also likely to move on to the next relationship just as easily.

Typically optimistic by nature, you don't expect a breakup or see the signs before it happens. It often takes you by surprise. But you're not always keen on giving up and may find yourself wanting to get back with someone who left you. The plus side to never giving up is that you're typically quick to bounce back after a breakup. Even if it does knock you down, you always know how to get back on your feet—after a brief emotional period in between, of course. You are pretty quick to move on, especially if you catch an interest in someone new. You may even instantly forget how broken up you were about your ex.

When dealing with a breakup, you should focus on clearing your mind. Yoga and meditation are good ways to start. You could also try motivational books. New sights and people can bring a sense of calm, so try traveling and sightseeing if you can.

Texting Back

You're the kind of person who, rather than texting back, will opt for calling the person who sent you the message. Why bother wasting the time to type out a long, extensive message when talking is just easier and faster? You tend to avoid long text conversations for the most part. Calling just makes more sense to you.

Choosing a Career

You're a Sagittarius, and as such, you may have a hard time settling on a career. You're too adventurous and spirited to want to stick to one thing for an extended period. You desire something new and need to remain stimulated and interested to remain in a career. Traditional jobs seem too dull for you to settle into. You have to be fulfilled to remain invested in your career. And one of the biggest things that gives you that feeling is helping others. You are also charming and are hardly ever insecure. This combination makes you well fit for a job as a teacher, mentor, or even a counselor. Bold and more than willing to take a few risks, you would thrive in a job that allows you to have a fluid and flexible schedule. A tedious job with a rigid structure will only bore you. Spontaneous jobs like flight attendant or journalist will allow you to explore and see the world while keeping things new and interesting.

Choosing a Major

There are quite a few choices when it comes to picking a good major for a Sagittarius. On one hand, you could opt for a degree in business. After all, working for an international company could take you to many new places. Or you could start your own business. Both give your free spirit the flexibility you need. On the opposite end of the spectrum, you could choose a degree in creative writing or photography. Getting to photograph whatever your heart desires, or having the ability to write when and where you want, are the kinds of fluid jobs that you would flourish in.

Study Tips

You have various interests and love to learn new things. This is something that you can use to your advantage when it comes to studying. Try to find interesting points that you can study and focus on. Make sure that you use a planner or schedule that will help you balance the various topics and subjects you need to study for. Using these tools will also help you to avoid stressing yourself out too much.

Attracting Wealth

You should be very cautious when it involves your finances and avoid taking too many risks. Instead, focus on being hard-working and dedicated. Make sure that you have steady control over your resources and be responsible when making decisions about your money. This includes ensuring that you have money set aside for a rainy day. Your wealth will improve with age, so stick to your dedication and be reasonable. You will be rewarded.

Winning an Argument

They don't get into arguments unless they know that they'll win. The best way to handle them is to test them. How well do they know their argument? Just because they think they know it all doesn't mean they have all the information. If you can prove that they're missing something, or you can show them that they're entirely wrong, they'll quickly shut down.

Dealing with Stress

You have a habit of just throwing yourself into things without really taking the time to plan them out first. Things typically tend to work out for you, but your luck will run out at some point, and sometimes things won't work the way you had hoped. You're often left floundering because your lack of a plan also leaves you with no escape route. Rather than trying to sort out how you're feeling, you try to escape by overly involving yourself in social situations. Plus, to keep up your persona, you tend to not divulge any of the stresses and worries you have to your friends. Or perhaps you'll try to go on an impromptu trip or vacation. Both are your ways of trying to escape instead of dealing with stress head-on. It's important that you actively handle these overwhelming feelings. Developing methods to combat stress and preventing future spirals will help you in the long run. Your mind and soul will thank you.

Boosting Your Confidence

You're a Sagittarius, so you're probably confident in yourself by default. However, you are not immune to questioning yourself which may cause your confidence to drop. Practicing positive thinking can easily boost your self-esteem right back up. Take a moment to look back and see just how far you've come in life. You've accomplished a lot, and you should have confidence that you will continue to accomplish great things. Just keep your focus on the things that make you happy and your mind will be more at ease.

Capricorn

Symbol: The sea goat
Dates: December 21 – January 20
Element: Earth
Modality: Cardinal
Ruling planet: Saturn

Capricorn traits
Full grown adult since age six
The responsible friend
Motivated by duty
Takes a while to warm up to people
Represses any emotion that gets in the way of success

Love

Capricorns often struggle in relationships because you have difficulty expressing how you're feeling. You also don't enjoy the idea of being emotionally dependent on another person. Even if you aren't as expressive as they may want, you tend to show care and affection in other ways. Capricorns highly value tradition and family. Thus, you can be pretty sentimental. Deep down, you have a desire to care for someone and build a life with them. It just may take time to realize that it's what your heart wants.

Handling a Breakup

You tend to have a reputation for being emotionless, even when it comes to breakups. You are very good at ending something when you know you want it ended, and you tend to give a nice clean cut in the process. If it isn't working, then it simply isn't working, and you're willing to accept that and move on whenever possible. Capricorns are not the kinds of people who try convincing someone to stay in a relationship with them. You prefer the practical and sensible, and in that mindset, you know that breakups are inevitably something everyone has to face. You tend to be more willing to face that fact so that you can move on.

Not usually one to casually date, you are more interested in investing your time and energy into a quality, serious, and long-term relationship. You don't have time to waste on people who aren't as dedicated to that ideal as you are. You are also more than willing to take on every challenge that comes with building a relationship. But Capricorns know their worth, and they're not ones to stick around when someone isn't giving the same amount of effort as they are. You'd rather be alone than be with someone who isn't worth your time. So, when you do have to handle a breakup, it can be very difficult for you to not dwell on it. You may see it as a failure, on your part or not, and become frustrated over wasted time. You're good at putting on a strong front, but behind the scenes, you wallow in your emotions alone. You might even bury yourself in work and projects to keep yourself busy, letting them consume you.

It's important to remember that you don't have to deal with what you're feeling all alone. It's okay to reach out to close friends and family. You're always there to help them, so now it's their turn to help you out. It will likely take you a while to move on. After all, you put so much into your relationship, and probably had all kinds of plans figured out and ready for the foreseeable future. Try not to dwell on it, even if it is frustrating and tiring. Instead, go out and try some new things. Visit new places, see sights with friends, and enjoy being spontaneous for a bit. It will help heal you.

Texting Back

You tend to be the kind of texter who falls within the middle of the spectrum. You don't reply instantly, but you don't take forever to answer either. You try to take enough time to come up with the best answer before you decide to reply. Plus, you don't want them to think you're waiting by your phone for a text.

Choosing a Career

You positively thrive in a position of power. You are focused on getting a job done, and getting it done well. And that is more than enough satisfaction for you. Your job doesn't need to be fulfilling to make you feel like you're accomplishing something. Once your mind is set on something, you'll get it done one way or another. As an earth sign, you seek out a sense of stability and structure when looking for a career. Jobs within businesses and offices are likely a perfect fit for you. You will likely prioritize success, productivity, and status, which makes you fit to climb the business ladder to the very top. People will respect the way that you handle things. Your dedication to getting the job done and speaking your mind will gain the admiration of your coworkers. Jobs that have a high amount of stress are perfect for you, as you will rarely ever crack under pressure.

Choosing a Major

Your analytical mind and need for a structured workspace are well fit for more science-based majors. Chemistry, for example, may give you the satisfaction you're looking for. Or if you would rather have a technologically-based degree, you can opt for majoring in computer science. Even engineering would suit you well. Any career you get from these degrees would give you the productive success you want and the consistency you need as a Capricorn.

Study Tips

Being a fairly practical person, you should use a similar approach when it comes to studying. Setting goals for yourself will help motivate you to get your work done. Once you reach them, you'll feel a sense of satisfaction and pride in yourself. You also tend to like competition. Setting up healthy contests between yourself and other students can help to fuel your motivation and desire to improve.

Attracting Wealth

You should try to emotionally remove yourself from worrying over finances, and instead, approach them with a more analytical mindset. Become part of various social circles, including joining clubs and organizations. This will attract abundance. However, if you're driven by selfishness, your finances will suffer, so ensure that you are fueled more by a humanitarian mindset. If your money views change, for better or worse, you will experience significant, abrupt shifts in wealth.

Winning an Argument

Capricorns are difficult to argue against. They are notorious for being very sound in their opinions, and they tend to have all the facts in line. So to win against them, you'll have to get down to the core of their argument. Remember to stay calm in the process. If you can prove that the baseline of their opinion is flawed, then all of their points are rendered useless.

Dealing with Stress

You are fairly well known for handling your stress exceptionally well. Sure, you feel the anxiety and pressure that everyone else faces. But you have developed an understanding that stress is simply a part of life. You work through it at the same calm, methodical pace at which you work through everything. You tend to handle your stress by yourself, and for the most part, you do a good job at it. But remember that it is okay for you to reach out for help from your friends. They will likely be more than willing to offer you any assistance they can manage. If you don't already, perhaps consider taking up some form of exercise. You tend to neglect your physical health whenever you're overwhelmed. If you make sure to take the time to work out, you will feel better physically and mentally.

Boosting Your Confidence

You tend to set pretty high expectations for yourself, which will naturally only lead to a loss of confidence. You prefer to have things planned out, and if they don't go that way or you're thrown out of your comfort zone, you may panic, which doesn't help your self-esteem much. A good way to help bring yourself back up is to find your favorite way of relieving stress. This can vary depending on your hobbies, but whatever helps to put your mind at ease would be useful. Also, actively remind yourself that you've got this. A few hiccups or a couple of things going awry doesn't mean the end of the world. You have the abilities and skills to figure it out.

Aquarius

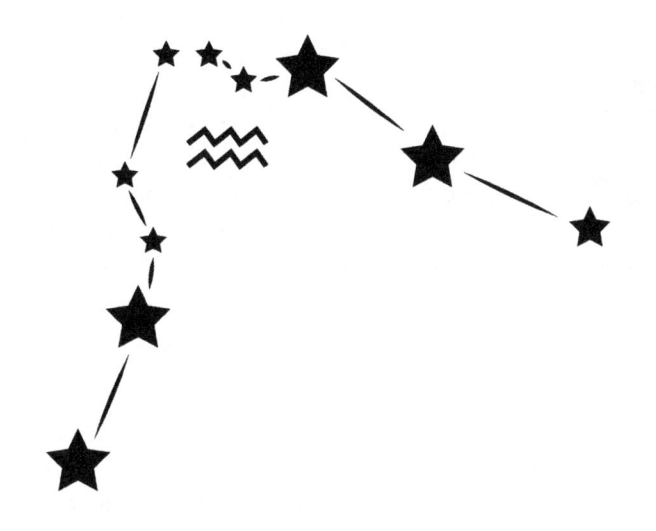

Symbol: The Water Bearer
Dates: January 19 – February 18
Element: Air
Modality: Fixed
Ruling planet: Uranus

Aquarius traits
Purposefully esoteric
Doesn't 'do' feelings, just concepts
Actually believes in conspiracy theories
More in love with humanity as a whole than individuals
Always feels like an outcast
Fetishizes personal freedom

Love

You don't often view romance as idealistic and warmly as most people do. To you, love is a philosophical pursuit, much like the other concepts that you have studied and grown to understand. You tend to be drawn to people who pique your interest. You don't want someone who shares your hobbies, but someone you can study and understand. You want to exchange knowledge with someone, expanding your mind in the process.

Handling a Breakup

You are a humanitarian at heart, and because of that, you don't tend to be troubled by relationship issues. You care about them, of course. But your mind is simply more focused on the issues of collective people. This can cause your relationships, and your feelings, to suffer. Your typical aloof and distant nature will come out during a breakup, whether you initiate it or not. After the split, you may find yourself analyzing everything that went wrong—and right—throughout the relationship. You might even look into studies or find other people who can back up your claims. To you, this is a way of coping.

Despite how calm and easygoing you try to be, a breakup will throw you for a loop. You may even find that you're physically expressing those negative feelings. You can become jittery and full of energy, leading you to run around trying to do as many tasks as possible to expel the feeling. You may talk endlessly about anything you can, but you won't acknowledge the real problem going on behind the scenes.

You need to stop and allow yourself to feel all the emotions you're avoiding. It may be difficult for you, as an Aquarius always struggles to handle their emotions, but it's important to your healing process. Maybe clear your head by going for a run, practicing yoga, or even letting out your frustrations in a productive way. Whatever you need to allow yourself to feel those sad feelings from your heartache is what you can try. Another thing to remember is to keep your friends around while you're healing. Or you can even volunteer, as making a difference always puts things into perspective for an Aquarius.

Texting Back

You're typically a very unreliable texter. Your friends probably don't count on you to answer their messages promptly. Sometimes, you can leave texts unanswered for weeks or even months at a time. If you do get around to responding to those long-ignored messages, you may start with a joke about your long absence. Hopefully, they know how you are and won't be offended by the silence.

Choosing a Career

As an Aquarius, you probably aren't too interested in the whole idea of settling into one career for the rest of your life. You don't want to be the kind of person who spends all of their free time working, and would rather work just enough to survive and spend the rest of your time pursuing your passions. You probably have more of an interest in volunteering than working. You want to make progressive changes, and your humanitarian heart and imaginative mind drive you to do what you can to make those changes. If you excel in math and sciences, perhaps finding a job within the field of technology is a good place to start. Doing so will allow you to develop positive and progressive change for generations to come. Otherwise, spending your time focused on doing what you can to bring change to your community will give you a feeling of satisfaction. But don't stop there. Your dedication and drive can bring about waves of positive change.

Choosing a Major

If you are an Aquarius seeking higher education, there are a few different majors that you may find yourself gravitating toward. Choosing a business degree is a good way to go, as it could give you the ability to found and build your own company one day. You could also go for a degree in education, as getting to mold the young minds of your students could give you a sense of purpose and leave you fulfilled. If you're more interested in finding a job that is completely out of the norm, maybe instead pick a major that fits that bill. Aviation is a possibility, as it will keep you far away from being stuck in a dull office job.

Study Tips

You tend to be a good student and studying isn't usually a problem for you. You're one of those rare kinds of people who can study well alone as well as in a group setting. It comes down to motivation. If you prefer to work out things alone, then stick to private study sessions. However, if you enjoy studying in groups, you should find a group that has similar motivations. Studying and working together can help you all to accomplish your goals.

Attracting Wealth

Don't focus too much on planning or budgeting your finances, or you will only deter wealth. Worry and stress over money won't help either. Instead, focus on having faith that wealth will come to you. There is enough for everyone, and believe that the universe will provide for you, and it will. Demonstrating a level of generosity with what you have will bring abundance to you in return. Let go of the desire to have a fortune and put your faith in the prosperity of the universe.

Winning an Argument

They tend to be too focused on the future and the big picture when forming their opinions. As such, their arguments can often ignore what's happening in the here and now. So, to win against them, you have to see what they aren't acknowledging. Counter their idealistic points with solid facts and sound evidence.

Dealing With Stress

You likely deal with stress constantly. As an Aquarius, you're always looking at the big picture, and rarely ever live in the current moment. Because of that, you tend to put things off repeatedly. And if you are dealing with a deadline, you can become overwhelmed quickly with anxiety and stress. You don't do well when backed into a corner. You don't like handling strong emotions, and may even dissociate to avoid feeling and processing them. You reach out to anyone you can for advice, but despite appreciating their different points of view, your stubbornness tends to lead you to handle it how you were originally going to. This pattern can cause you to feel isolated and as though no one understands what you're experiencing. One way to handle this is to chat with strangers. Fresh, new perspectives may be just what you need, as they can open your eyes in a way that your friends and family cannot.

Boosting Your Confidence

You are a fluid person, and change doesn't bother you much. But we all have moments where we question ourselves. When you're feeling like this, remind yourself that you are the kind of person your friends come to for advice. You always see the bigger picture in life and have probably opened many eyes and hearts when giving advice. If you're looking for a boost, put yourself in social situations. Being around your friends and meeting new people will help to lift your confidence back up. You'll start to feel like yourself in no time!

Pisces

Symbol: The fishes
Dates: February 18 – March 20
Element: Water
Modality: Mutable
Ruling planet: Neptune

PISCES TRAITS
Somehow both 5 and 50 years old at once
Thinks everything is a sign
Can't remember if they dreamt it or it actually happened
Excessively romantic
Prone to fantasy
No boundaries

Love

A dreamy, empathetic, and idealistic person, you can be very charming to those interested in your open heart. You often seek the feeling of love and enjoy the idea of being surrounded by it. But you tend to lose yourself in your partner, believing that love is the melding of two beings into one. This can cause relationships to be difficult for you, as you can attract partners who take advantage of this. You need someone who understands the boundaries of a relationship and is willing to help you to establish your own.

Handling a Breakup

Your high level of empathy can be a blessing and a curse when it comes to relationships. It may be easy for you to get overwhelmed by emotions when you're in a difficult situation, and you could find yourself fleeing to avoid it. When it comes to breakups, you prefer to keep them indirect, vague, and oftentimes confusing. Rather than deal with the emotional confrontation of a split, you would rather be able to move on fluidly from one relationship to the next.

Despite your level of sensitivity, you are one of the signs that can handle a breakup a bit better than most. And that is due to your "old soul." You are naturally resilient and hardened, able to survive some of the toughest situations. You may appear sensitive and fragile, and others expect you to crumble in difficult situations. But your strength is settled deep into your soul, which aids you in things like breakups. It also allows you to help those around you who may be going through their breakups. This tendency to help others also means that you may struggle to reach out whenever you are emotionally distraught. It's okay to go to your friends for help and support.

Another key to your healing process is ensuring that you stay socially active. Spending time around positive people will help to uplift you when you're feeling down. Dwelling on it too long may only cause you to develop a negative mindset, which will keep you from healing and poison your spirit. Venting productively can expel those feelings, and help keep you from believing that the world is against you. Find something else, such as a pet or your friends, to pour your love and affections into. Your nurturing heart will feel more at ease.

Texting Back

If the conversation you're having is enjoyable, you'll be extremely fast at replying. You love talking about topics that you enjoy. But this focus won't last forever. You may lose interest and be quickly distracted by something else, even leaving texts half answered. At that point, it's just not entertaining to you anymore, and you probably won't get around to answering at all.

Choosing a Career

You have a profound level of empathy and are incredibly intuitive and observant by nature. You're capable of a lot of things if your heart and mind are set to it. Your ability to understand people is second to none and, as such, you may thrive as a therapist or counselor of some kind, especially if you are inclined to help others. On the other hand, exploration may be more your thing. Whether it be exploring the nature of the mind as a psychologist or the far reaches of space as an astronaut, you will be up for it. Your interest and dedication to something is based on the mission itself, rather than the money you can get from it. You tend to avoid positions of power and don't prefer leadership roles. But that doesn't mean that you wouldn't do well in them. Your ability to understand people and their motives and your openness to new and creative methods would work well in management. However, make sure to avoid jobs that are naturally competitive or driven based on money and profit. You will not thrive in places like that.

Choosing a Major

If you are more of a creative-minded Pisces, perhaps majoring in photography will fit you. Not only are you able to express yourself, but you would also have a knack for bringing warmth and ease to the subjects of your art thanks to your innate nature. Or you can go for a degree in fashion design. You have a knack for seeing things that others don't and you could bring a new vision to the industry. If you're not creatively inclined, perhaps you could major in psychology. Not only do you have much empathy and a desire to help others, but you also have a craving for exploration, making the many jobs that this degree could offer some great picks for you.

Study Tips

You likely have a hard time sitting down and studying, often finding yourself daydreaming instead of working. This is especially true when the classes are focused on analytical and factual information. You'd much rather be exploring creative and fun topics. Try to find a quiet place to study and put distractions away so that you can focus. Also, set goals for yourself, even if they are small and incremental. You are fueled by motivation, so accomplishing goals and rewarding yourself is the best way to tackle hard-to-enjoy studies.

Attracting Wealth

You have to be the kind of person who takes action to attract wealth to you. You probably have all sorts of ideas and plans for how you can make money. Make sure that you put these ideas into motion, or you will never achieve the income you desire. Don't delay your plans or worry about them not working out. Be adventurous enough to take the first step. Taking risks can reward you significantly. Try out new things and don't settle for the same old ideas. Your creative mind can bring you significantly more wealth.

Winning an Argument

Not only are they sometimes too kind for their own good, but Pisces' arguments can often be impractical and unrealistic. To win against them, you have to force them to see the reality of the situation. Bring them back to earth with the facts, even if you have to be blunt about it. Find the impractical parts of their points and they won't know how to react.

Dealing with Stress

As a Pisces, you likely handle your stress fairly well. You are intuitive by nature, and rather than letting all of your anxieties pile up, you're able to get to the very root of an issue fairly quickly. You have a knack for understanding your stresses as though you're an outsider looking in. To cope with your stress, you tend to go for spontaneous changes. You're likely to get a new tattoo or piercing, a whole new wardrobe, or dye your hair a new color whenever you're feeling overwhelmed. You see your outward appearance as a method of escapism. When there are things you can't control, at least you can change the things you can. You have a habit of entirely separating yourself from what you're dealing with, but in the same breath, are more than willing to help a friend in need. While very admirable, it's important to remember that your needs matter as well. Ensure that you are taking care of your mental and physical well-being so that you feel prepared enough to tackle your anxieties.

Boosting Your Confidence

You have a habit of holding onto things from the past and letting them follow you into the present, weighing your confidence down. The best way to lift it back up is to remind yourself to let go of those things. They're in the past for a reason. You'll feel so much lighter if you loosen your grip on them. Remind yourself that you are a strong person. Another way to boost your confidence is to embrace the art forms you enjoy. As a Pisces, you are artistic by nature, so indulging in that will lift your self-esteem. Also, focus on building strong and lasting relationships with the people you care about. Having a close group of friends with whom you have a deep connection will also help your self-esteem quite a bit.

Conclusion

Astrology is an expansive and sometimes overwhelming topic, but learning about it will surely bring you a sense of peace and understanding within yourself. While this book is not intended to teach you every possible thing there is to learn, it should give you the perfect starting point to delve deeper into the heavens. Having a good grasp of basic terminology and influences can make clearing up the mysteries much easier.

Remember that you are far more than just your Sun Sign. You have a sky full of influences, and each factor is important to you and your future. You should be able to interpret some basic parts of your chart with the tools within this book. But don't stop there. Many online sources can help you to further unlock the truth behind your Birth Chart. With how different everyone is, it's impossible to include each detail within these pages. The next step is up to you.

Whether you are investigating your astrological influences or someone else's, you should have a better understanding of how they can be altered so drastically and influence people so heavily. No matter the reason, you chose to read through this book to begin your journey to exploring astrology on a more profound level. The cosmos are calling for you to expand your heart and mind. Best of luck in reaching the higher self that you're searching for

From the Author

Thank you very much for taking the time to read this book. I hope it positively impacts your life in ways you can't even imagine.

If you have a minute to spare, I would really appreciate a few words on the site where you bought it.

Honest feedbacks help readers find the right book for their needs!

Bless you,

Olivia Smith

Made in the USA
Middletown, DE
01 April 2022